What the reviewers are saying about

"Grant Teaff has [...] affair with life, his fe[...] football, a beautiful wi[...] [...]. There are no Xs and Os, just a lot of joy and a few tears as Teaff tells his life story.

"This book is destined to be a best-seller."

—Dallas Times Herald

"As a rule, I do not care for inspirational books, but in the case of Grant Teaff's *I Believe*, I'll make an exception.

"This is the story of how a young Christian football coach moved from a small state college to salvage the failing football program at Baylor University. . . . How he did it is remarkable, and the book itself is a course in self-motivation."

—Atlanta Journal/Constitution

" 'I believe that God has a plan, a purpose, and a will for every life,' Coach Grant Teaff states at the beginning of this fascinating account of his life.

"This thrilling account of Baylor's miraculous climb to its first SWC title since 1924 is for anyone, whether you're a dyed-in-the-wool football fan or not."

—Shreveport Times

"No book could have been titled more accurately than this book. This is the story of a man who does believe. He believes in God. He believes in his family. He believes in the athletes under his direction. And he believes in himself.

"Football enthusiasts will find this account fascinating, but one needn't be an expert to enjoy every chapter. This book and the adventures related herein are well worth reading."

—Lawton, Oklahoma
Constitution

"Although this book is the story of Baylor University football coach Grant Teaff, it is not another run-of-the-mill jock memoir.

"Laced with humorous anecdotes and behind-the-scoreboard life and thoughts of a football coach, Teaff's story is a wellspring of excitement and inspiration for persons of all ages."

—*Dallas Morning News*

"The strength of this book is not in the types of football plays described or the strategy of a winning coach, but in the teachings about life and how an individual should relate to others and to God."

—*Jackson Sun*

GRANT TEAFF
I BELIEVE

with
Sam Blair

A Key-Word Book

WORD BOOKS
Publisher
Waco, Texas

First Printing—August 1975
Second Printing—December 1975
First Key-Word edition—September 1976

I BELIEVE

ISBN: 0-87680-832-1
Library of Congress catalog card number: 75-19893
Printed in the United States of America

To

Donell, a perfect wife, who happens to be
                                    my best friend
Tammy, Tracy, Layne, who make me proud
                                    to be a father
Bill and Inez Teaff, whose son could not have asked
                                    for better parents
A loving God, who gave life, friends, opportunity
                                    and all that I have

Contents

Introduction

Grant Teaff is a man who radiates some wonderful human qualities: a loving concern for people, a quiet confidence in others as well as himself and an unflagging desire to do the best he possibly can in anything he undertakes.

He is a football coach who achieved unprecedented success at Baylor University, one who clearly knows the X's and O's. More importantly, he is one who knows the heart and soul.

That is why the impact of his career, and his life, reaches far beyond the scoreboard. As significant as it has been athletically, it has been even greater spiritually.

Perhaps no school anywhere could appreciate the Teaff touch as much as Baylor. If ever there was a place which needed his special talents, this was it. Although Baylor is the largest Baptist university in the world and could lay legitimate claim to many proud distinctions, it was burdened by a king-sized complex about its football history when Grant arrived in 1972. The Bears had not won a Southwest Conference championship since 1924, and that bugged a lot of people. He changed that, which was fine, but what really was great was what his program and personality did for their pride.

9

After they made it to the top in 1974, there was a new awareness of who they were and what they stood for. Baylor people everywhere seemed to glow, and so did the campus.

Located in the Central Texas city of Waco, 100 miles south of Dallas and its sophisticated church-related university, Southern Methodist, and 100 miles north of state capital Austin and the awesome home campus of the University of Texas, Baylor for years generally was considered old-fashioned and out of step. Liberal observers scoffed at its strong ties to the Baptist church, although it's unlikely any other situation might exist at a university owned by the Baptist General Convention of Texas. Baylor, it seemed, just wasn't with it.

The combination of a championship team and its coach's charisma made the Baylor style more appealing. There was a new respect for the type of Christian education offered on its campus. New dormitories, modern classroom buildings and laboratories with the latest equipment stretched down to the marina on the Brazos River, although sentimental "exes" assured architectural reminiscences of an earlier day when they forced the restoration of condemned Old Main and Burleson Hall, beloved turn-of-the-century landmarks. Sure, Baylor still was different but people had a new appreciation of it.

Baylor, with an enrollment of more than 8,000 students, is Texas's oldest university in continuous existence. Founded in 1845 with one teacher and one building in the small town of Independence, it really began to prosper after its move to the thriving city of Waco on the Brazos, a river the Spaniards originally named Los Brazos de Dios—"The Arms of God." As college football became a major sport in the United States, Baylor fielded a number of good teams. Trouble was, they usually weren't quite good enough.

After the Bears won their second championship in three years in 1924 that incredible drouth set in. During the next forty-nine seasons Baylor certainly had its share of poor teams, but there also were times it proved quite competitive. In twenty of those seasons it finished second or third in the Southwest Conference race. The result was an air of frustration which hardly made for an ideal coaching climate.

The ten-year career of John Bridgers was a perfect example. He became Baylor's head coach in 1959 and produced exciting, interesting teams good enough to play in bowl games during three of his first five years. The championship always eluded him, however, and he never commanded the full support of the Baylor people. The division grew along with the disillusionment until Bridgers was fired at the end of the 1968 season.

Bill Beall followed for three dismal seasons, and by the time athletic director Jack Patterson hired a little-known coach named Grant Teaff, 1924 seemed more like 1824 to the Baylor faithful. But soon it became apparent to these people as well as the general public that Teaff was a rare one, a skillful coach of great emotion and feeling and deep religious beliefs. His personality, warm and friendly and positive, attracted people. His words held them.

"Baylor needed that special person who could mix with all classes of people," Patterson said. "He has to be at ease with everyone, and Grant is. He could go into a bar with a group of coaches and the others could drink all they wanted and Grant would not be out of place. He could still enjoy the association, but a lot of men couldn't do that. Then he could cross the street to a Baptist church, go into the pulpit and deliver an outstanding sermon."

John Stevens, director of a tremendously moving film featuring Teaff and shot at Baylor in the fall of 1973 for the Southern Baptist Radio-TV Commission, has been a fan of his since.

"On a scale of 1 to 10," said Stevens, "he's 10. He doesn't set out to impress you. He just does."

John Scovell, who played quarterback at Texas Tech while Teaff was an assistant coach there, also had a special view. "Grant Teaff," he noted, "is the best I've ever seen one-on-one, whether he's talking to a 65-year-old or a green kid."

"Grant has great humility," Patterson noted. "When he lost some hard ones he suffered but his first concern always was for the players and for Baylor. When he won some big ones he rejoiced but his first concern still was for the players and Baylor. He thinks of everyone else and puts himself at the bottom. That's pretty unusual in successful men.

"He's a tireless individual and a good organizer. His coaches practically idolize him and that carries over to the players."

In an era when many coaches and other well-known people insist on unlisted telephone numbers, Baylor's Coach of the Year continued to be listed in the Waco directory. And the name of Grant Teaff was clearly displayed on the mailbox at the curb in front of his home. He is an open person and the lady of the house proudly tells the world her husband is genuine.

"He is the man," said Donell Teaff, "whose image you see."

Grant Teaff has been hailed as Baylor's man for all seasons. And he is, for many reasons.

Sam Blair

1.

The Greatest Victory

Although not quite thirty years old, Grant Teaff was beginning his fourth season as head football coach at McMurry College in the fall of 1963. He expected it to be one of unusual stress and strain. Less than a month before practice opened he had been stunned by the news that the school was eliminating athletic scholarships. This crippled the program which Teaff and his staff had worked to build. The prospect of keeping talented athletes or recruiting new ones without scholarships was dark, and no one would have blamed Teaff for leaving quickly and not risking damage to his promising career. But he decided to stick with the players who stuck with McMurry.

On a strange Saturday night at Monroe, La., they learned a togetherness that few people can ever know, and it happened after the game had ended. The date was Sept. 28, 1963.

I believe that God has a plan, a purpose, and a will for every life. I accepted Jesus Christ when I was twelve years old, just a small boy in Snyder, Texas, but it was some years later that I began to understand that a God who would love me enough to send his Son to die an earthly death—an excruciatingly painful death on a cross—would not put me on this earth without a plan, a purpose, and a will for my life. I was never totally and firmly convinced of this until that night McMurry played Northeast Louisiana.

We had flown to Monroe on a twin-engine DC-3 operated by American Flyers, a charter service based in Fort Worth. Our traveling party consisted of twenty-eight players and three coaches, plus the two pilots and the stewardess. It was a fine trip and we were excited about the game. Despite the shock of losing our scholarship program we had been competitive in our first two games, winning one and losing the other by only four points. We wanted to make this a special season in the history of McMurry College football.

We played well against Northeast Louisiana and led 7–0 late into the fourth quarter. With less than two minutes to play, Northeast Louisiana had the ball on our 40–yard line. Then came the big play which apparently assured us of victory.

Their quarterback sprinted outside left end on the run–pass option, cut upfield for five yards and then one of our linebackers really smacked him. The ball popped loose, rolled another five yards forward and our safety covered it.

We were whooping and jumping on the sidelines. We knew we could run out the clock from there. But suddenly we saw the officials' red flags flying.

There was a confusing conference on the field. Then the referee took the ball back to the line of scrimmage, stepped off five yards against Northeast Louisiana and signaled illegal forward pass. They got a penalty but kept the ball! It was an incredible ruling on a play which clearly was a fumble and had wound up in our possession. Everyone from McMurry blew his stack but it did no good. We lost our poise and Northeast Louisiana would up winning the game. They scored a touchdown three plays later, made the 2–point conversion and went ahead 8–7. We were finished.

In the dressing room everyone was very mad and upset about losing the game the way we had. I settled down and began talking to the players. I told them we had played well enough to

win and that if we would go on with the same attitude, somewhere down the line we'd win a big ball game that we weren't
supposed to win. In fact, I told them, "You'll win the biggest
game of your life when you're not supposed to win it."

We showered, dressed, went by a restaurant and ate chicken-
fried steak with lots of gravy and French fries. Then we boarded
our bus and headed for the airport.

The plane was in a position at the end of the runway where
it looked like we wouldn't have to taxi out for takeoff but the
crew wasn't there. We loaded our equipment and then took our
seats. Still no crew.

We were sitting there fuming about losing and wanting to
get the heck back to Abilene when we saw the headlights of a
taxicab shining outside the plane. The pilots and the stewardess
jumped out and rushed on the plane. I guess they had been
having a good time somewhere and lost track of the time. The
pilots shut the door to their cabin and started the engines. In
their haste they failed to go through the complete check-list
prior to takeoff. They revved up the engines and in a moment
the plane started moving down the runway.

I sat there fuming about the loss, looking out the left front
window. I always sit in that seat and look out the window. I'm
glad to get off the ground and glad to get back on it. But that
night I noticed something strange. We were moving at a good
speed, fast enough for takeoff, but the plane didn't leave the
ground. We were getting dangerously close to the end of the
runway.

Suddenly I felt the plane lurch upward. The groan of the two
engines was almost deafening but we were off the ground,
skimming above the lights at the end of the runway and moving upward very slowly. We nearly touched the tops of the
telephone poles and suddenly the propellers clipped the tops
of some pine trees.

The pilots slowly turned the plane and circled over the city
of Monroe. They were heading back for a landing. None of us
knew it, but the pilots had come to the stark realization the
moment they tried to lift off the ground that the elevators on
the tail section were still locked. When we arrived for the game

they had placed clamps on the elevators to keep them from moving in the wind while the plane was parked. In their rush that night they had failed to take them off. Miraculously, we had gotten into the air without good control of the plane, but the pilots knew we had to get back on the ground.

They attempted the landing and I thought we were finished. When they decreased the power the nose of the plane dipped drastically. We hit the ground, bounced back into the air and the plane turned sideways. I just knew we were going to flip wingtip over wingtip.

A picture flashed into my mind of that horrible crash of the Cal Poly team several years earlier. Many of the players and coaches died a fiery death in that one. Was that to be our fate?

But somehow the plane righted itself. The groaning engines droned on and we pulled upward into the sky. The pilots circled the city again and attempted a second landing, but this time with no decrease in power. They approached the runway at something like 150 miles per hour. Suddenly we touched down, but we were only on one wheel! That's when we learned the left landing gear had been completely destroyed, the tire blown out, and the gear bent, on our first attempted landing.

So now we were teetering on one wheel down the runway, the left wing dipped and its tip almost touched the ground. The props hit the asphalt runway, sparks flew but somehow the pilots righted the plane, pulled the nose up and shot the power to it. Suddenly we were airborne again.

We were circling Monroe a third time and I guarantee you there were a lot of white knuckles in that cabin. Then the door to the pilots' cabin opened and the captain came back.

He wanted to tell us we had a problem.

He informed us that the elevators were locked, the left landing gear was destroyed, the electrical system had been damaged, and that we were loaded with fuel. "We have only one alternative," he said, "and that is to fly to the Strategic Air Command base at Shreveport and try a belly landing."

I said, "Well, what are we talking about then? Let's get on our way."

It was about thirty minutes flying time to Barksdale Air Force

Base. We sat there in total darkness, not knowing if we were flying at ten feet or 10,000. The captain came back again and said we needed to move some of our weight back to the tail of the plane to help our chances for a belly landing. I asked the other two coaches, Buddy Fornes and Herschel Kimbrell, if they would move back there with me. We groped our way to the rear and sat down on the floor. As we listened to the engines groaning in total darkness it was very, very quiet in that cabin.

Suddenly one of the players called out, "Coach Teaff, would you lead us in prayer? We're all pretty frightened."

I stood up, my hands resting on the last seats on each side of the aisle, bowed my head and prayed as fervently as I've ever prayed in my life. I came right out and asked God for the lives of the young men, the coaching staff, and the crew of that airplane. And somewhere in my prayer I said, "Surely, God, you have a plan, a purpose, and a will for our lives. We pray, God, that it not end on this night."

I sat down on the floor again. It was very uncomfortable. I was behind the last two seats, my back bent out slightly toward the rear of the plane. I sat there in the silent darkness thinking how very few times in our lives that we face death—and know it. Actually, we face death every moment because we have no guarantee of drawing another breath. Life could end in an instant but we never think of that. Here was an opportunity to think about death in a real way. We were going into that Strategic Air Command base loaded with fuel, and a crash landing meant the possibility of fire.

I sat there and thought about my life. I thought about my wife Donell and my two daughters, Tammy and Tracy, both very young. I thought about my Christian life. I guess one always thinks of God when death is near but I thought about my life as a Christian, the acceptance of Christ as my personal Savior, and how little I had done in the ensuing years in my relationship and growth toward God. I thought about my job: the opportunity to work with young men, to have what you say and do be meaningful in a very great and warm way. I didn't want to die. I promised myself and, in turn, God, that if I were to live through this that I would be different. A different person, husband, father, coach, and above all, a different Christian.

When we were about ten minutes out the pilots yelled back into our compartment, the stewardess asked the coaches to help the players get in the proper position for a crash landing. They dropped their heads between their legs, leaned forward in their seats, and then we pulled pillows and blankets from the upper racks and placed them around their heads. We checked to be sure all loose items were safely stowed, then we took our seats in the rear of the plane and waited for the crash.

The pilots took the plane down to about three feet off the ground, pulled the workable landing gear up and shut off the power. They had radioed Barksdale after leaving Monroe, explained our plight and asked that the runway be foamed down to aid a crash landing. But the split-second the fuselage touched the runway we knew there was no foam. There was the screeching, tearing sound of metal on concrete and sparks engulfed the plane. The right prop dug into the concrete, tore away from the plane and sailed off into space. The right engine burst into flames and the right wing started to burn. We bounced through the air on first contact, flew a little way, hit the ground and bounced again, then hit a third time and began to drag and slide along the runway. The plan turned slightly to its right, then slightly to its left and then suddenly came to a stop.

Buddy Fornes kicked open the back door of the plane and we started unloading the players. One player walked up the aisle holding the stewardess in his arms. Suddenly I saw the pilots working their way outside as quickly as they could. I thought that strange because there still were passengers on the plane, but they were hurrying outside to pull the locks off the elevators before the investigators arrived.

By the time we got everybody off the plane safely the firemen had come and put out the fire. The plane was a wreck, a terrible mess. The fire chief said he'd never seen a plane so hot fail to explode.

I called the players and said, "Men, let's kneel and in a prayer of thanksgiving thank God for our deliverance." We knelt and I led the prayer but it wasn't nearly as fervent as it should have been. It seems our prayers of asking are always more fervent than our prayers of thanksgiving.

Suddenly someone tapped me on the shoulder. It was an air policeman. "Are you in charge of this group?" he asked. I told him I was and he gave me sort of an odd look. "I hate to tell you this but you are under arrest." I asked on what charges. "Illegal entry into a Strategic Air Command base," he said. "It's a formality but we have to do it."

"That's fine," I told him, "as long as you don't line us up and shoot us."

Soon we were on buses and heading off the base to the Ramada Inn in Shreveport. I checked all the players into rooms after inspecting them for injuries. We didn't have a one, not even a scratch. One young man who had sat in the seat nearest the right wing and had seen the engine explode was a little shaken up psychologically, though.

We put them all in bed and then I spent most of the night on the phone, answering calls from families of our players and the news media. The story had spread across the nation that the McMurry football team had survived not one opportunity to die but four.

On Sunday morning a plane flew in from Fort Worth to pick us up and the president of American Flyers charter service was the pilot. After breakfast they bused us back to the base to board the plane. I've never been on a plane before or since that had thirty-one complete inspections from front to back. Everything was checked out by each player and coach.

A couple of players wanted to ride the bus back to Abilene but I persuaded them to get on the plane. One young man pulled his helmet from the equipment bag and carried it on the plane. The minute they started the engines he strapped it on. I thought about doing that myself but it does look a little odd.

When we landed at the airport in Abilene we were met by a crowd of well-wishers and the news media. There was so much to talk about, so many questions to answer, that the afternoon went by rapidly.

That evening, as usual, our family went to our little church,

Southwest Park Baptist. Our pastor was Brother Earl Sherman, a very strong Christian man with deep convictions. Brother Sherman preached a wonderful message that night, a very brief one, and it centered on the fact that he believed with all his heart that God had spared the lives of the McMurry coaches and players because he had a plan, a purpose, and a will for our lives.

Suddenly my own words and the thoughts that had gone through my mind on the plane and my own prayers leaped at me. I was bursting with emotion. I jumped from our pew and ran out of the church.

It was about a mile up a hill from the church to our field house at McMurry. I ran all the way. My hand trembled as I took the key and opened the door, rushed through our dressing room and then into the meeting room. I turned on a light, then turned it off and went back into the dressing room. I couldn't hold back the tears. I fell on my knees and finally in that room that I loved so much I thanked God very deeply and fervently for our deliverance, and for the fact that he had spared our lives in a miraculous manner.

I said, "God, I know that you have a plan, a purpose, and a will for my life and for the lives of these young men. I do not know what it is but I'll spend the rest of my life trying to find your will and your purpose for me. And I'll also try to impress upon the young men that I coach this year and forever that there's more to life than just playing football; that you do have a plan . . . a purpose for our lives."

I went home and found Donell very worried about me. I told her about my feelings, my emotions, and my thoughts. The next morning I talked to Coach Kimbrell and Coach Fornes about the way I felt. That afternoon I called a squad meeting and I related to the squad my exact feelings about our experience and what I believed it meant.

One player said, "Coach Teaff, we've gone through this unusual experience together. Why couldn't we form a club and some years hence hold a reunion and see what God has done with each of our lives?"

"That's a great idea," I said. "On the 25th anniversary of the crash we'll get together and see what has happened to us."

Another player said, "Coach, this has been a harrowing experience. Could we name the club something fun?"

"Great," I said, "and I'll tell you what I'll do. I'll have cards printed with the name of the club and we can all be card-carrying members of this club. Every time we look in our bill-folds and see those cards we'll be reminded that God spared our lives and that we have a plan and a purpose."

One player who had been in deep thought spoke up. "I have the perfect name for our club," he said. "Since we're the Mc-Murry College Indians, let's call ourselves the Brotherhood of Indian Belly-Landing Experts." Everyone in the room laughed.

I said, "Hey! That's a long name but I think it's a great one. How do you guys feel?" They all yelled their approval.

Another young man said, "Coach Teaff, why don't you have a Scripture put on the cards that always will remind us of this experience?" Everyone liked that idea, too.

That afternoon I went to a printer and told him what I wanted. McMurry wore maroon and white but the closest we could get to a maroon card was red. So I said, "Well, that's great. We'll print it on red and everybody will know that it's supposed to be maroon." He laughed and asked me, "What else do you want on the card?" I told him we wanted a Bible verse, the name of McMurry College and the date of the crash. "Which verse do you want, Coach?" he asked me.

"I'm sorry, but I have no idea," I told him. "Do you know a good Bible verse?" He said, "No, but I have a Bible here. Take it and find a verse."

He handed me the Bible and I nervously opened it to Romans. I put my finger on the page just to start reading to see if I could find something appropriate. I found myself in chapter 8 and my finger squarely on verse 31.

It said, "What shall we then say to these things? If God be for us, who can be against us?"

"Use that," I told the printer.

I was most pleased when I left because I had found someone

who could print the cards quickly, and because I had found with such ease a verse that would mean so much to all of us involved in that experience. The next day I went by after lunch to pick up the cards. They were wrapped in brown paper and I didn't open them. I just took the package to our dressing room and waited for the players to arrive. I was wondering what I might say to them when I presented the cards.

Nothing really had come to mind when I heard the players gathering for our meeting. I walked in with the package in my right hand and said, "Fellows, at your request I had the cards printed. I found the Bible verse and found it a very unusual way and I want to tell you about it because I think it further emphasizes the point that God has made in all our lives: that God is real and that he has a plan and a purpose for us."

After I explained it, I handed the package of cards to a young man on my right and asked him to open them and pass them out. As he circulated them, all of the players looked at their cards in amazement.

"Coach Teaff," one player said, "the name has been changed."

"Oh," I said, "I forgot to tell you. The printer called and said the name was too long and he wanted to abbreviate it. I told him fine, because we all knew what it meant."

The player said, "Coach, the abbreviation turned out to be B.I.B.L.E. We have formed the Bible Club."

Just one more signal that God was saying something to all of us. Since that time a well-worn card has been in my billfold in my hip pocket. I've told this story to thousands of people and every time I tell it it touches deep into their hearts because it's stranger than any fiction. It's true.

In Romans 12:1-2, there are the words of Paul, who I think was one of the most dynamic persons ever to live. Not large in stature, but very powerful and dynamic. Paul said, "I beseech you my brothers to offer yourselves as a living sacrifice, dedicated and acceptable in his sight. You can no longer conform to the modern-day trends. You must let your mind be remade and when your mind is changed your whole nature will be transformed. Then you will be able to understand that which is perfect, that which is acceptable, God's will."

I've never seen anything written in flaming fire across the sky pertaining to God's will for my life, but I think as we go through life that we have certain feelings. We know when we are right with God and that we are moving in the direction he would like for us to go. I knew without question that I was supposed to go to Baylor University. Too many things transpired, too many things happened. I also believe that during this span of years I am supposed to be at Baylor.

I do not know what God holds for me in the future but I know one thing, I will strive to find God's will and plan for my life. I know it is difficult for a lot of people to reach this conclusion. But I wish you could take my word and not have to experience what I did to understand that God does love you enough that he has a wonderful plan and purpose for your life.

On April 22, 1966, another American Flyers charter, carrying Army recruits from Fort Benning, Ga., to Fort Ord, California, crashed into a hillside sixteen miles northeast of Ardmore, Oklahoma. Of the 98 persons aboard, 82 died.

The pilot was Reed Pigman, the president of American Flyers who flew to Shreveport on September 28, 1963, and took the McMurry football party safely back to Abilene.

2.

Believing, and Loving

On January 9, 1975, the American Football Coaches Association voted Grant Teaff "Coach of the Year" for the 1974 season. His selection was not surprising. Baylor's remarkable climb from the Southwest Conference cellar in '73 to the school's first championship in fifty years had been a national story for weeks. NCAA records showed the Bears to be the most improved team in major college football from the standpoint of victories, rising from a 2–9 record in '73 to 8–3 in '74. The job which Teaff masterminded was the talk of the coaching profession.

Now coaches everywhere wanted to hear him talk and they weren't disappointed. He became the featured speaker at Coach of the Year Clinics across the nation. In a two-month period Teaff addressed a total of 35,000 coaches in such cities as Boston, Pittsburgh, Atlanta, Chicago, St. Louis, Oklahoma City, Dallas, Minneapolis, Grand Rapids, and Kansas City. During a whirlwind weekend on the West Coast in mid-February he spoke at four clinics and, as usual, received rave notices at each stop.

When he rose to speak to an audience of 1,400 at

the Jack Tar Hotel in San Francisco on Saturday morning February 15 he was operating on a very tight schedule. He had flown in from Seattle late the night before and had attended a Fellowship of Christian Athletes breakfast before his clinic appearance. He would have to leave as soon as he finished his talk to fulfill his commitments to clinics in Los Angeles and Santa Monica. He was moving at a hectic pace but loving it. He told the audience his trip was worthwhile if one person came away with something beneficial and useable in his own life.

His talk was preceded by high praise from Duffy Daugherty, who had directed Coach of the Year Clinics since 1959. "Grant Teaff," said Daugherty, "is the finest clinic speaker I've ever heard."

Becoming national Coach of the Year was one of the great thrills of my life. I guess every coach would aspire to be elected to this honor by his peers. I humbly accepted it and I think it probably meant more to me than perhaps anybody who's ever received it.

I've been in the valley many, many times, as you have been, and I'm sure I will be there again. But the experience of the mountaintop has been a great pleasure. I hope that in some way all of you who love coaching will be recognized by your peers. I hope you understand that Grant Teaff being selected simply means anybody in this country is capable of attaining that lofty position. I'm just happy that Baylor University shared in it with me because it knows about those valleys, too.

We have developed a loyalty there which I'll always cherish. I believe with all my heart that one of the greatest qualities of human life is loyalty. I wouldn't have a man on my coaching staff who is not loyal to me, to the program, or to my school. If you don't have a capacity for loyalty, you're a loser and you'll always be a loser. You find me a person who has loyalty and dedication and I'll show you a winner.

When I first went to Baylor everybody said, "Hey, man, that's a loser. You're throwing away a good career to go there.

There's no way you can win." But I believed you could and I took the job. It was a tremendous challenge but I believed it could be met by establishing a strong and constant program of motivation.

Motivation simply is a force, tangible, intangible, or sometimes both, which propels someone into action. It is the most vital part of human life. Therefore, motivation is the key to success. It can be developed through several methods.

There's the "boss" method. This is the authoritarian method of motivation and there's nothing wrong with it if you use it properly.

During the '74 season at Baylor we received tremendous national publicity which basically said, "Grant Teaff is a great disciplinarian." Well, that's not necessarily so.

That publicity came about because we saw to it on a college level that players were in bed at eleven o'clock every night except before a game, and then earlier, and we made it compulsory for them to be up at seven o'clock every morning and eat breakfast. It was "boss" motivation but there was a reason I dictated this particular discipline.

It all reverts back to goals, which are a tremendous part of my life. I couldn't live without them. They're also a part of each player and coach in our program.

Baylor hadn't had a winning season in eleven years and hadn't won a championship in fifty, but before the '74 season we set our goal to have a winning season and to play in a bowl, even if it were the Chili Bowl. That's a high and mighty goal under those circumstances but our players set it and they believed in it. And it's important that you let them set the goals. If they're your goals they're not going to attain them.

I knew the goal was high because our schedule included seven teams which at some time during the season ranked 12th or higher in the nation. We had lost our last seven games in '73 and weren't supposed to win one in '74. Sure, a winning season was a lofty goal for us.

We didn't say we were going to win a championship. That goal came later. Realistically, you have to crawl before you can walk and walk before you can run. So why in the world talk about a championship when you haven't had a winning season in eleven years?

I said, "Okay, I believe you can have a winning season and play in a bowl but how are you going to attain this goal?"

Someone said, "First of all, coach, we're going to have to be bigger. Everybody on our schedule has a tremendous weight advantage against us. We'll have to be more physical."

I said, "Great! How are you going to do it?"

"Well, coach," someone said, "we have a fine off-season weight training program and a developmental running program that will help us in the spring. In the summer we'll have to work extra hard and come back for fall practice in proper physical condition. Then we'll have to stay with our weight program throughout the season."

So they stayed with it and our squad averaged a gain of eight pounds per man from the beginning to the end of the season. Instead of tailing off at the end we were growing stronger and more physical.

But that spring when we set our goals we still needed to find ways to make the plan function. One player said, "Rest is real important. We should get in bed early but that's hard to do in a dorm. Somebody wants to visit awhile, you study awhile, watch a late TV show and it's one o'clock before you turn out the lights."

So, we put them in bed at eleven o'clock.

You may say you can't tell college athletes when to be in bed and I say, "Hogwash!" However, you can't expect them to get in bed on their own.

One of our coaches visited the dorm each night to make sure they were there with the lights out, and ready to go to sleep. But it never got heavy-handed. Instead, it opened up some beautiful new communication between players and coaches because it offered a relaxed time when they could talk about anything they wished.

One of the players also said, "Nutritionally, breakfast is the most important meal of the entire day. We'll just have to make a pact that we'll all get up and eat breakfast."

I agreed, but then we made sure they did it. Naturally, there were complaints. "But, coach, I don't have a class until ten o'clock!" "Tough," I said. "After breakfast you can study for two hours. You've been lying in the sack, sleeping through your ten o'clock class, too, and you're flunking."

We raised the football players' grade average 10 percent. They were more alert. They were stronger as the day went on and we had better workouts and practices because they started their day rested and properly fed.

Sure, that was a type of "boss" motivation but there were a lot of angles to it.

There's also the "good ol' boy" method. You know, "The kids won out there because I'm a good ol' boy."

I like people and I hope people like me. It's my nature to be a good ol' boy. But I'll tell you one thing: I'd rather have a player's respect than have him like me. If I can have his respect, then soon he will like me. I believe this feeling can be a motivating factor but you shouldn't expect it to be the lasting basis of your relationship. If it is deeper and has more meaning than that, then it can be a great motivational force.

Sportswriters and coaches across the country said some wonderful things about what happened at Baylor, but the greatest thing said on my behalf in 1974 was when a sportswriter asked one of our players, "Why does this team play with such determination, dedication, effort, and polish game after game?" And that young man told him, "Simply because Coach Teaff expects it of us and we don't want to disappoint him."

Man, that's the greatest thing that's ever been said! I'll always remember and appreciate it.

A third method is "tricky" motivation and I plead guilty to having used it. Not in recent years but early in my head coaching career at McMurry College. I wasn't much older than some of the players and I thought I knew everything there was to know about coaching. I thought the tricky method was part of it.

There is some place for it, I guess, because it once helped us beat Arlington State, a much larger school which was heavily favored over McMurry in our homecoming game.

About ten o'clock that Saturday morning we had finished our pre-game meal and the players gathered in the meeting room. It was my last chance to tell them something great to get them ready for the game. Just before I went through the double doors into the room I saw our mascot, an old cur dog named Ringer, dragging around the corner. He was white and the first week he showed up around the locker room some guys painted black shoe polish around his eye and called him Ringer. Every day they would feed him something from the cafeteria and he had free run of the dorm, sleeping in any room he wished. He became just like one of the players.

But ol' Ringer was in bad shape now. He was staggering and weaving so I called him over to me. Evidently Ringer had been out chasing a little girl dog, wound up fighting with her boyfriend and didn't fare too well. His left ear looked like it was hanging by just a few threads. There was a big gash right down the middle of his back with blood oozing out, and a big hunk of fur was gone from his hip like somebody had plucked it right out of him. Ol' Ringer was looking for sympathy. Suddenly, the tricky approach to motivation hit me.

I picked him up, gently nuzzled him to my chest, then backed off from those double doors and came at them with a bang. I stepped into the room holding Ringer and the doors swayed behind me. The players looked up, startled. I walked to a long table in front of the players and laid ol' Ringer on it. He was doing a heck of a job, rolling his eyes and whining.

I said, "Fellows, last night those people from Arlington came in here and got hold of ol' Ringer. Just look at him!"

It was phony, and looking back I know it was awfully corny, but those players responded to it. I never saw a bunch more highly motivated. They played so well that afternoon we beat Arlington State by 20 points.

Afterward Chena Gilstrap, the great coach from Arlington, came across to shake my hand. "Coach," he told me, "that was a magnificent job. But I can't understand why they were playing so wildly and viciously."

"Well, Chena," I said, "let's just say they won one for the Ringer."

Then there's the "reward" approach to motivation. While it

has meaning it also is not something you can build on permanently.

All of us are motivated by tangibles. We have to eat, sleep, and drink so we're motivated by those things. All of us desire to have certain needs and pleasures fulfilled but if that's all you're motivated by you're in a heap of trouble. If a person's not in the coaching profession for deeper reasons than that, he'll be gone in two or three years. But if he's motivated by deep personal commitments rather than tangible things then he'll be in coaching for a long time.

I believe we must have self-motivation. Each of us has a "hot button" and if we learn how to press it and propel ourselves into action then we can be motivated individuals.

I am self-motivated. I don't have to wait for somebody else to push my hot button. We had better learn what turns us on. Then, as we work with people we can learn what turns them on and teach them to press their own hot buttons.

If I have to motivate a team week after week it will not grow and succeed. That team is made up of individuals with different concepts, thoughts, and ideas. If I try the same thing on each team, totally, it's not going to work. There are certain basics you must know and understand if you're going to teach people to motivate themselves. I like to put them on five levels, like stairsteps.

First is food, liquid, work, rest, recreation—our basic needs for physical, tangible things.

Second are safety and security needs. You'll never know how many young men join you because you have a solid, sound program. Maybe for the first time in their lives they can find safety in your leadership and direction, security in numbers.

Third is the need for affection, the feeling of belonging. Everyone desires to be loved and to love. Unfortunately, too often in life we fail to show affection. I don't let a day go by that I don't tell my players that I love them. Sometimes it's tough. I may say, "You guys are driving me crazy, but I love you."

A beautiful thing happened to me in 1973 when we were

losing so much. A young black player walked up to me after a game when I was feeling terrible. He weighed about 250 pounds and he put those big arms around me and nearly squeezed me in two. "Coach Teaff," he said, "I love you!"

Man, I tell you that loss and all of our heartaches and tears somehow diminished in that moment. They didn't seem nearly as important because one human being cared and said he did.

How long has it been since you told your mate, "I love you!"? Try it! Go home and say, "I love you!" when you walk in the door. Call your children to you and tell them, "Hey, you little rascals, I sure do love you!" You do, so why don't you tell them? Love, affection and belonging are such vital parts of human existence.

Fourth is the ego, or self-esteem, need. Self-confidence is important to all of us, and appreciation certainly is.

I played for a coach in college whom I loved and respected but that guy never showed any appreciation for anything I did. I was all-conference tackle, all-conference linebacker, team captain and student body president. But not one time did he ever say, "Hey, Grant, you're doing a great job!"

After my last game, when we'd won the conference title and he had been elected Coach of the Year, I was standing by my locker when, wham! Someone hit me on the tail. I turned and there was my coach. He winked, smiled, and walked away. I tell you, that was worth a million dollars. But why hadn't he done it earlier? If you feel it, show it! You never know when some young man might become self-motivated by your appreciation.

The fifth and highest step is self-fulfillment. This is most important because it deals with your self-development, the total of what you want to become. And nobody in the world knows what you want except you.

To be fulfilled you must have goals in all areas of your life, not just in sports. Financially, socially, spiritually, mentally, physically, you must set immediate goals, then intermediate goals, then ultimate goals. I believe it is important to write them down. Every coach and player in the Baylor program lists his goals on a 5-by-7 card which I place in a file. Each one of them comes in my office twice a year and we sit down and talk about these goals.

I want to know if one of my coaches wishes to become a head coach so I can better help him achieve it. And I want to know the individual goals of different players. Of course, in some cases I have found it necessary to remind them what they are.

One young man left some goals with me which I thought were great. But the next spring I had a report from the dormitory that he was tearing up the place and had a terrible attitude about everything. I called him in, handed him his card and said, "Read me the top line." "Ultimate Goal: I want to be a head coach at a high school in Texas and after my third year win a state championship."

He looked up and our eyes met. "With your attitude and conduct in the dormitory," I said, "how do you expect to attain that goal? You're not going to be a member of this football team, you're not even going to be in school here if all of this doesn't change."

He said, "Well, coach, I never really thought about it." I said, "Well, think about it!" Thankfully, he did. There never was one more problem with him. In fact, he was one of the captains on our championship team in '74. He was able to see further than the end of his nose but he had to be urged to look. 90 percent of your discipline problems occur with guys who say, "Well, I didn't think." Make 'em think!

Early in 1974 Aubrey Schulz handed me his goal card. He was a reserve lineman who weighed only 210 pounds and didn't play enough to letter as a junior in '73 when we were 2-9. I looked at his card and said, "Aubrey, you have a high goal here." He said, "Yes, sir, I sure do." "I see where you want to be all-Southwest Conference center next season." "Yes, sir, I sure do." "That's strange since you play guard." "Yes, sir, I know, but I want to play center and I thought if I put it among my goals that you would . . . ah . . . would . . . ah . . . change me." I said, "Okay. We'll think about it."

I looked again and saw another goal. It was, of all things, to be all-American center! Then I looked and saw a third goal: To help lead Baylor to a conference championship!

We hadn't been conference champions in fifty years and didn't win a conference game in 1973, and he's going to lead us to a championship! Well, I'm as positive as anybody but I thought that was a little unrealistic. But I didn't say so. I started talking to him about how he was going to attain these goals.

First of all, I told him he must gain a lot of weight. "If you're playing center when we open at Oklahoma next September you'll have to block a nose guard who weighs 250 pounds. Everyone else through the schedule will be as big or bigger, going up to 290, Louie Kelcher at SMU."

He said, "Coach, I want to play. I want to win. I'll do whatever it takes." Well, we put him on a training program and I've never seen a guy work harder. In spring practice he became our starting center but he still weighed only 218 pounds. He kept working on the program though and I told him to call me in the middle of the summer and tell me how he was doing. He had a job in a pizza restaurant and he tried to eat all the pizza there. He did everything to gain weight. He called me and said, "Coach Teaff, you won't believe it but I weigh 221!" I said, "Three pounds. That's great! That's advancement! Come on in bigger." "Yes, sir," he said.

When we started 2-a-day workouts in the fall he weighed 223. He was fantastic. I've never seen anybody work any harder, develop techniques any better. We opened with Oklahoma and after the game their starting nose guard was benched. Next week at Missouri we lost again in the fourth quarter but he played great. Then we came home to play Oklahoma State, eighth-ranked in the nation and with a 280-pound nose guard. Aubrey now weighed 229 pounds and he whipped him all over the field. We won by 17 points.

The rest of the season we lost one game. We won the Southwest Conference championship and Aubrey Schulz, who was considered the eighth best center in an eight-team league in September, was the unanimous choice for all-Southwest Conference. And when the Football Writers of America named their all-America squad, Aubrey Schulz was first team. Even more fantastic, after we ended the regular season November 30 by beating Rice to clinch the championship, I put him on the scales. He weighed 245 pounds.

I'll never see a better example of a guy bringing his goals alive. Aubrey Schulz decided where he wanted to go and he was able to put wheels to those goals. He worked and he attained. Self-fulfillment: the fifth and top level of motivation. It's tremendous.

There are certain things which I believe aid self-motivation in people. Communication is first. By communication I mean more than just talk. I mean eye-to-eye contact and *listening*. You can't be thinking about what you're going to say next. Listen to what the other person is saying so you can understand.

Confidentiality is very important. I saw a coach once try to be confidential with a player and the player really responded to it, telling him some things deep inside of him. Then two weeks later the coach took those things and pulled them out, trying in some way to motivate other players and coaches. He lost that player forever. When someone comes to you in confidence whatever is shared should remain in confidence.

One must also have a positive attitude about life if he is to help others to grow. Don't ruin yourself by being around people who are negative and always thinking bad thoughts. If you're around them enough you're going to become negative because input turns into output. Whether in the coaching profession, business, or whatever, if you're negative you're gone. I like to offer people a positive thought which they can take and apply to their own lives. It's very simple:

"I am only one, but I am one. I can't do everything, but I can do something. That which I can do, I ought to do. And that which I ought to do, by God's grace, I can do."

Yes, I am only one, but I *am one*, created in the image of God and with the ability to act and to think and to do. Be proud of who you are, what you are and do something with it!

I love the words of that TV commercial: "There's nobody else in the whole human race with your kind of style, your kind of grace. There's nobody else like you!"

Nobody else like you, with your challenge to do what you

can with the talent and ability you have and then to give the credit and glory to God. Whatever you do, you do by God's grace. Give him the credit because I believe that man's relationship with God is the most important human involvement. Treasure it, and nourish it.

You must develop belief. Don't get involved in something just because somebody else is doing it. Make application to what you are, who you are, and who you have working for you. Then choose what is right for you and go with it. Then you can develop belief. And you must be solid in your beliefs.

First, believe in yourself. Take all the information you can gather and sift it down to a point where you can use it. Now you have self-confidence. Next help those around you believe in themselves. That's not easy sometimes. They've been banged around and never had a victory and you've got to develop a little belief in them. Let them learn to believe in others. Believe in them and they in turn believe in you, in themselves, and in their community.

The third facet of belief—the most important one—is your belief in God. You're made up of the mental, physical, and spiritual qualities of life. Picture your life resting on a tripod with those qualities providing the legs. If you have only the mental and physical qualities, the thing would fall over. At Baylor we try to create an atmosphere where a guy can feel free to grow spiritually. This is not crammed down anyone's throat. We place it before the men and they decide what it's worth to them. Through the Fellowship of Christian Athletes we allow them to grow at their own rate of development. And when you believe, you grow. It's beautiful!

You must always be aware of individual worth, including your own. At one clinic a coach walked up to me and said, "I'm just a junior high school coach but . . ." "Wait a minute!" I said. "Listen, man, there's nobody in the coaching profession more important than a junior high coach. I believe the most important coach today is the guy who works with those young people in their formative years of junior high age. Don't ever say you're *just* a junior high coach."

Remember that. Nobody is *just* anything—unless you think you are.

Care can make a great difference in whatever you do. It's been said the coaching staff at Baylor cares and I don't think a greater compliment could be paid us. You can't counterfeit care. It's something very valid and very important.

All of us respond to success and you must remember everyone needs it. I believe little successes lead to major successes. The little successes can be found everywhere. I go out during practice and check our drills; if I see a guy getting whipped time after time I change the drill around so he can win. I don't want him ever to leave the field after a workout without a victory under his belt.

One's mental approach is fantastically important, because if a person is not right mentally there is no way he can find his hot button nor can you. At Baylor we develop the mental approach with a calculated coolness.

In staff meeting on Mondays we make up a game plan for the entire week concerning the mental approach we want to take. Every day of that week we have a word or group of words that lead toward the game and our theme for that week.

Against Oklahoma you might think our theme was to go up there and whip Number One. Well, it wasn't. Our theme was confidence, simple confidence.

We went to win but if we did not win we wanted to come away from that football game with some confidence. Well, we played the heck out of them for three quarters, trailing only 7-5 and in the fourth quarter they finally beat us 28-11. But we were competitive against the classiest team in the country. We gained confidence. On the trip back to Waco we knew 1974 would be a much better season for Baylor.

The mental preparation had begun on Monday, when the key word was "knowledge." There's no way you can have confidence without knowledge. You must know what you're doing, know your teammates, and know your opponents. Each coach in his individual group work put his own interpretation to the word "knowledge" and at the end of the workout I called the squad together and put the capper on it, my own interpretation of that particular key word.

Next day it was "commitment." You can't gain confidence, respectability, or a championship without a commitment to a cause. On Wednesday the key word was "conditioning." I guess no team in the country worked harder on conditioning— and it paid off. Throughout the season we emphasized conditioning, hard work, development, proper rest, and nutrition. The players understood it. Conditioning is part of your confidence.

On Thursday the key word was simply "believe." Believe in yourself, in each other, in God, and believe that something good is going to happen to you. On Friday morning we flew to Oklahoma and we were right mentally. On Saturday afternoon we were all right on the field. We were 43-point underdogs yet we expected something good to happen to us. It did. We came away with respect nationally and confidence in ourselves.

It was the beginning of a wonderful year for everyone at Baylor, because we believed.

The San Francisco audience which had greeted him with polite, respectful applause when he was introduced roared its appreciation when he finished. Grant told the coaches they would next see a fifteen-minute film based on a week in his life during the '73 season, one which led to a 34–28 loss to TCU. At the time it seemed a miserable experience but one which proved to be a wonderful inspiration when the finished film was seen in the fall of '74. He apologized for having to leave and not visit with them personally after the film but he left them as he did all the coaches he addressed with these parting words: "God bless each of you and I love every one of you."

The response to his Coach of the Year appearances was tremendous. Coaches across the country wrote to thank him for the experience.

"When you see grown men standing in adulation with tears in their eyes," wrote Bobb Troppmann, manager of the San Francisco clinic, "you have to realize that your message reached home. I am proud of you, and to quote Grant Teaff, 'I love you.' "

"I have never written a letter of congratulations to a speaker," said Richard Cerone of Classical High School in Lynn, Massachusetts, "but your inspirational presentation has moved me to do so."

"It was the finest lecture I have heard in 25 years of attending coaching clinics," said Jimmy Maffett of Macon County, Georgia, High School.

"The coaches in attendance," said Joe Broeker of Pacific Lutheran University, Tacoma, Washington, "needed to see and hear from a program that truly believes in kids and desires to provide creative fulfillment rather than exploiting them for a Saturday afternoon win."

"You made me take a long look at my life," said Ernest Lewis of Pittsburgh, "and have helped me find ways in which I may improve myself as a person."

"Coach Teaff," said Don Patrick of Newton-Conover, N.C., High School, "you are a winner, 10–0 or 0–10."

"You have established something that is somewhat indescribable," said Dave Handy of Thompson Academy, South Boston, Massachusetts, "and that no one can take away. I thank you for that small part you shared with me."

"I wish," said Chuck McKelvie of Fall River Mills, California, "that you could speak to every high school kid in America."

"You've done a lot to help me and we've never

even met," said Richard Tyner of Grapevine, Texas, High School, "but the greatest thing I admire about you is what you have done for Baylor University." (Tyner graduated from TCU.)

"You are the first major college coach I've heard," said Harold Beach, a Southern California high school coach, "who emphasized the reality of Our Lord in coaching. I really appreciated the emphasis you placed on the spiritual gap that needs to be filled as we coach our young athletes."

"Many of the things you spoke of I will remember for a long time," said Larry Curtis of Forest Hills Northern High School, Grand Rapids, Michigan. "I only hope those goals and ideals will become a part of my life."

"It was the most meaningful presentation I've heard in my coaching career," said Richard Yobst of Salisbury, Maryland, State College. "Sincerity, love, honesty, and concern for those around you and your job came through in a most understandable manner."

"I was very happy for college football and Baylor University to see you win the Southwest Conference title," said Dick James of Ventura, California, College. "Your kind of Cinderella story brings hope and reality to every athletic program in the country."

"I hope when my son grows up," said Paul Baviello, another Southern California high school coach, "he has the privilege of playing for a man like you."

One group of five coaches was so impressed by Teaff and Baylor that they devoted their Easter vacation to a five-day round trip by car from California to

Waco in order to visit for a few hours. Among them
was Lou Randall, a young man who had experienced
a great change in his life.

I had learned through a letter from one of his friends, Larry
Stevens, that Lou had accepted Christ after hearing me speak at
the Santa Monica clinic, and that through Lou's influence another coach at Garden Grove High School, Gene Campbell, had
accepted Christ. He wrote that this was having a profound effect
on their entire school. When they arrived for their visit, however, Lou wasn't aware that I knew about his experience. After
a group meeting, he stopped me in the hall and asked me in a
rather quivering voice if he could talk to me alone. We went in
my office and I closed the door.

He opened his mouth and nothing came out. He began to cry.
I suspected what was on his mind because of that letter but I
waited for him to talk.

Finally he said, "I just wanted to tell you personally what
you've meant to my life. When I sat at the clinic in Santa Monica
there were 1,400 coaches in the audience but I knew you were
talking directly to me. I went home that night and I couldn't
sleep. I lay in bed and cried all night. Finally, the next morning
I accepted Christ. My wife thought I had gone crazy but three
or four days later she accepted Christ, too."

By then he could talk all right and he was bubbling. He
talked about the response they had had in their school among the
players and coaches.

I talked to him about how this part was easy, really, kind of
like winning a game and feeling so great about it. I said what
you must be conscious of in your Christian experience are the
tough times. A lot of people make the wrong assumption about
accepting Christ. They think the minute you do that your problems are over and everything is perfect from then on. That's not
so. You're going to have sinking spells and everything won't go
as you'd like in your life or your career.

"It's amazing that you say that," he told me. "I'm also a baseball coach and we haven't won a game since I accepted Christ."

I told him about my experience in '73 when we lost nine

games. Before we played Texas I was interviewed by a preacher on his thirty-minute prime time TV show. One of his questions was, "If you're a so-called Christian coach at a so-called Christian institution and you have a majority of so-called Christian players, why in the world doesn't God let you win football games?"

My answer to him was that I didn't believe God really cared too much about football games. That God really cared about individuals who play football games. Football games are won on the line of scrimmage by athletes. If an athlete has a relationship with God I think he can be a better athlete, just as such a relationship can improve you in any endeavor. But just being a Christian doesn't insure victory in football or business or anything else.

I think that helped Lou Randall quite a bit. He understood that becoming a Christian doesn't necessarily solve all your problems, but it can help you meet those problems and try to overcome them.

That visit was an interesting experience and a gratifying one. To see something like that evolve from a talk at a coaching clinic proved without a question that God can use just about anything if it is given and received in a proper manner. That never ceases to amaze me.

3.

A Home with Heart

People are a precious commodity with Grant Teaff. His deep feeling and rare understanding of others began in a hometown as typical of West Texas as a sandstorm.

Snyder, located about ninety miles southeast of Lubbock, is a thriving city of 12,000 which takes understandable pride in its prosperity and achievements. Once it wasn't half as large nor nearly as prosperous, but in the summer of 1949 it became Boomtown, USA, the center of a great oil discovery.

The new wealth changed the face of Snyder, bringing modern homes, schools, parks, and a more aggressive business atmosphere to what once was basically a cotton-farming and ranching community. But it didn't change its heart. Today when Grant Teaff visits his hometown he still feels the warmth of his boyhood.

I always have loved to observe people, seeing how they behave, react, and what makes them tick. I have seen people who had so much in the way of worldly goods and yet really had so little. And I have seen others who lived modestly but knew the riches of a full life.

As a boy I spent a lot of time around the Stinson Motor Company, an auto agency, gas station, garage, bus station, truck stop, and tourist court where my dad worked. He's very personable and he built a strong business through his personal relationships with the people who traded there. One person I've never forgotten was a wealthy man, who owned one of the biggest ranches in West Texas.

A towering man who wore expensive black suits and smoked big cigars, he had a world of material possessions. His land, outside of Snyder, contained some 300 active oil wells and he lived in a large house. But despite this, I always felt sorry for him because his life seemed to lack a special dimension.

During the 1920s he allowed an incident to alienate him from the people of Snyder. He had come into town in his Model T and had a wreck on the city square. The other party sued him and he got so upset that he swore he'd never go into town again. Well, my dad's place was three or four blocks from the square and that's as far as he ever went. Dad would get his groceries, go to the bank and post office for him and take care of any other business he had in Snyder. When Dad had finished, this man, a bachelor, would get in his car and drive back to his ranch, alone. It seemed so strange that someone would hold a grudge and let it detract from his own happiness. It was sad to watch him, a man who didn't have a family and who really didn't have a town.

There was my dad, who had only a high school education and worked very hard for a modest income, but was so involved with life and people. And then there was this rancher, wealthy but lonely. This taught me that a person's worth and value cannot be determined solely by educational or financial circumstances. No matter what your background, the individual is what's important.

My dad always has been a tremendous football fan. I couldn't guess how many thousands of miles he has driven to watch me play or coach. I was about six when he started taking me to the Snyder High games and I was immediately fascinated by the excitement that people felt for football. Snyder was a typical West Texas town in that respect. Everything revolved around the games on Friday night.

They painted their car windows with "Beat Rotan" or "Beat Merkel" and if the game was out of town they'd form a caravan and hit that highway.

In a town like ours the players were a big attraction. An even bigger attraction was the coach. As soon as I knew anything about athletics, when I was about thirteen, I decided that coaching was the life for me.

The coach had a tremendous influence on the people around him and he received a lot of respect from the community. I wasn't interested in material things but personal relationships meant a lot to me and I really admired the opportunity the coach had to bring people together, teach the players, and inspire the fans.

Grant Garland Teaff was the first child born to William Garland Teaff and his wife, the former Ruby Inez Grant. Bill Teaff was trying to make a living as a tenant farmer when Grant was born Nov. 12, 1933, in their little house near Hermleigh, ten miles outside Snyder. In those Depression days it wasn't unusual for babies to be born at home.

The Teaffs soon moved to Snyder, where Bill worked in a cotton gin for awhile and also spent some time with the WPA, the federal government's program to create work for jobless men in the '30s. He worked on road crews for ten cents an hour and later became a foreman at $1 per day. None of these jobs offered any hope of steady work, however, and in 1937 he hitchhiked across the South Plains in search of something more solid. He found nothing and late one night caught a ride back into Snyder and stopped at the Stinson Motor Company's all-night gas station. He heard some heartening news. A man had quit there that day.

My dad showed up at six the next morning and just started waiting on cars, fixing flats, servicing the bus, doing whatever needed to be done. He worked all day and the next morning showed up again. Finally Mr. Stinson walked up to him and asked, "What are you doing here? I'm not paying you." Dad said, "I know that but I thought if I could show you I'm a good worker if you ever had an opening you'd put me on." So Mr. Stinson told him, "Anybody with that kind of drive I'm going to give a job." He started Dad at $18 a week and Dad worked ten straight years, sixteen hours one day and 12 hours the next, without one day off. He wound up part owner of the business.

The way he got that job always impressed me and has become part of my philosophy. I never worry about salary or anything like that as long as my family's taken care of, because I believe if you do the job things will take care of themselves. Dad told me when I was very young, "Anything worth doing is worth doing right."

We were a close family despite Dad working so much. Any time he wasn't at his job he spent with us. There was love and happiness and ours was a Christian home. Both my parents had grown up in the Baptist church. Dad was never a deacon or a real heavy church worker but he's a good Christian man. He was working seven days a week so Mother took my sister Juanez, who's six years younger, and me to First Baptist Church, where she has taught the same Sunday school class for third grade boys for more than thirty years. It was a tough day for me when I was promoted and had to leave her class.

Mom is soft-spoken, kind and patient but she's also very determined. And she has a wonderfully optimistic nature which I must have inherited from her. "I'm pessimistic," Bill Teaff once laughed, "but Inez always thinks we're going to win, even after we've lost the game. We went to Waco for the Texas game in '74 and when Baylor was behind 24–7 at the half I was ready to drive back to Snyder." (Baylor won 34–24.) She loves people, so she thrives on the job she's had for years selling shoes in Gene Thompson's store on the courthouse square. Like Dad, she wants to stay involved.

At sixty-five he was still going strong as superintendent of maintenance for Texaco in Snyder. He came to Dallas to see our Cotton Bowl game with Penn State on New Year's Day, drove 275 miles home that night and went to work at five o'clock the next morning.

Teaff is an unusual name and any time you see one in this country you can be sure we're related. We're all descendants from a clan of gunsmiths who came from Germany with General Von Steuben, a soldier of fortune and mercenary who fought for America in the Revolution. My ancestors settled in what became known as Steubenville, Ohio. There still are some Teaffs in Steubenville and I've visited with them but they pronounce their name with the long "a"—"Tafe."

The Teaff I descended from moved to Virginia and then to Yellville, Arkansas, a pretty little place up in the hills. He had ten or eleven sons and they moved into various parts of Texas. I descended from one who lived around Bell County in Central Texas. So while it's an unusual name we have Teaffs all over. But there never will be enough of us, I guess, that everyone will know how to pronounce and spell it.

My ancestors may have been big on guns but I never was. Still every little kid went bird hunting with his B-B gun, trying to shoot them out from under the eaves of the house, and I did, too. I remember the first one I killed. When I picked that bird up I realized it was a little creature who had died for no reason at all. I never cared to do that again.

I love the outdoors and I often went to my uncle's farm. A few years later when I was about twelve I wound up with a single-shot .22 and somehow rabbit hunting seemed the thing to do. I walked through the woods and a cottontail stopped right in the trail in front of me: the perfect shot for the perfect hunter. I raised my rifle and drew a bead but then that little rabbit turned and looked at me with those big eyes. I just dropped my rifle and shooed the rabbit away.

When I went back to the house my aunt asked me, "Did you shoot anything?" I said, "Oh, yeah, I got me a cottontail out there in the woods." I felt any boy should brag about being a hunter, but I knew I'd never be one.

I never really traveled until I got into college so I grew up figuring all the world looked like Snyder. I thought everybody ate dirt and the wind blew strong in your face and your hair

never stayed combed and water was scarce. I taught myself to
float in a little concrete tank in a neighbor's backyard but I
didn't really learn to swim until I was in college. I had been
coaching four or five years before I ever wore my hair more
than three-quarters of an inch long. Of course, flat-tops were
stylish then but in West Texas you cropped your hair close because of the wind.

In the really dry years tumbleweeds blew through the town
and you'd see them piled up against the fencerows out in the
country and the sand would drift. My dad never liked farming
because he suffered too many dry years. That was before we
had irrigation in that part of the country and it was just tough
old work with precious few rewards.

Although I went to church regularly I wasn't "churchy" at
all. Church to me was a social thing. Throughout my boyhood,
high school, and college days I didn't get too involved with the
religious aspect of it. I accepted Christ at the age of twelve and
I was baptized but I can't say it was like a bolt of lightning
striking at my feet. I didn't change drastically. I was still the
same ratty little old kid. I never did anything really bad but I
didn't go around with a halo over my head.

There's no question that Christ touched my life then but at
that time God was up there and I was down here. I knew there
was going to be some connection but I didn't know what my
end of the deal was.

There was some variety in the social life. Besides church and
football games, there were picture shows, rodeos, dances and
pool halls.

I was a pretty good horseman and I'd ride in the rodeo pa-
rades, wearing my cowboy hat, boots, Levis, and hand-tooled
belt decorated with "Teaff" and three red roses. The rodeos
were fun and so were the dances after them, except for one
when I was about fifteen or sixteen. It was the only time I ever
got drunk.

My good friend, who was a little more worldly than I, said,
"I'm going to fix us something called a Salty Dog. You're really
going to like it!"

Of course, a Salty Dog is grapefruit juice with a lot of salt and gin in it but I think he used vodka because it doesn't have much of a taste. We went out to the car and drank some and I said, "Man, that's good!" It was salty and the more I drank the more I wanted—kind of like eating peanuts.

We'd dance awhile and go drink some more of that Salty Dog. Whew-ee! I was really out of it. Everything got blurred and I was sick. That stuff ruined my whole night. I missed the fun and felt awful. That's one of the reasons I decided early in life that I didn't like alcohol.

But I liked pool very much. There were two pool halls in Snyder, on opposite corners of the square and both in the basement. We'd go there and shoot snooker, pool, and play the pinball machines. It was fun and I never learned anything bad. Now we have a pinball machine in our home for our girls to play. We don't have enough room for a regular pool table but we do have a bumper pool table and they enjoy it.

I always had spending money because I started earning it when I was eight delivering the Snyder Daily News. From the paper route I moved into doing jobs around the garage for my dad, fixing flats and washing cars. By the time I was twelve I was working with big truck and tractor tires. This was during the rationing of World War II and I had to crawl around and check the serial numbers of everybody's tires. I fixed truck flats although some of those tires were almost as big as I was.

I was still twelve when I started working weekends in the grocery store next to the station, from eight in the morning until midnight. I have a vivid memory of that job because about seven o'clock one Saturday night I saw my dad pull up in front of the store in a shiny black Model T, grinning ear to ear. He had bought it for $75 from a widow who had it put on blocks in her garage after her husband died. It was in mint condition, with a nice canvas top and a rumble seat that pulled up in back. That was my first car.

I became something of a social happening around Snyder because of it. I always had a car after that and I loved to haul a load of kids around. A year or so later I got my grandmother's Chevrolet coupe and I found a new adventure—driving the railroad tracks to Roscoe.

We were at the tail end of the R, S, and P. The Roscoe, Snyder, and Pacific. It simply carried freight about thirty miles back and forth between Snyder and Roscoe, where it joined two main lines. We knew the schedule for the train and we'd get my car on the tracks between runs. We'd let some air out of the tires so the car would settle down right on the rails, then put it in gear, lock the foot feed and sit back. We really felt grand out there on our own railroad.

The oil boom hit during the summer between my sophomore and junior years in high school. Suddenly Snyder went from a sleepy little town to a place throbbing with excitement. There was a strange new atmosphere. People and machinery came in from everywhere. The population shot to about 20,000 and oil well supply houses cropped up for several miles out on the highway.

The demand for living space was incredible. People were sleeping everywhere—in old barracks, warehouses, under the stands of the football stadium. Some people ran dormitories in three shifts around the clock. You got off work, came in and paid for a bed for eight hours. They set an alarm clock and when it went off they got you out so somebody else could get in.

Snyder is the Scurry County seat and we had a great old courthouse with spires and turrets and lots of gingerbread on it. I climbed to the top of it one evening and counted 285 oil wells in a complete circle around town.

That boom brought a different type of people to Snyder. One street became known as Skid Row. So many people in the oil fields were heavy drinkers and when they couldn't get rooms they'd just pass out in the street. I'll never forget driving along and seeing them stretched out everywhere, sleeping it off.

The people who had lived there didn't change, though. I always admired the people around Snyder who came into a lot of money during that time because they did stay the same. Nobody became snobbish or all caught up in it. For many it only changed their life style gradually. They didn't rush out and build a huge mansion like they did in '*Giant*.' Today they're the same good country people they always were. That impressed me. I hope I would have been the same had that happened to us.

There was no real athletic background on either side of my family. Dad played a little football for his community team at Knox City when he was in high school and that was it. He's not a big man, about 5-10 and 155 or 160 pounds. Mother was one of three daughters who lost their father when she was very young and she had no contact with sports when she was growing up in Knapp, another little place near Snyder. She's a small-boned woman and only stands about 5-4. Of course, when I got my full growth and was playing college football I was over six feet and about 200 pounds. I guess I got my size from my dad's uncles, some of whom stood 6-5 and 6-6. When I played for Snyder High, though, I never weighed more than 151 pounds.

I was slow, too. I really didn't have a lot of athletic skill but I wanted desperately to play. I wanted to be a part of that team, to know the admiration and respect which I felt for the older players. I didn't mind hitting people on the football field. That's where I developed the theory that to block and tackle effectively you must lead with your face. Of course, you paid a price for it in the late '40s and early '50s because there were no face masks on the helmets. The coaches always said I'd stick my face in there and I've got the flat nose to prove it. It was broken eight times.

My freshman year I hurt my left knee but didn't have surgery. That knee still locks today, meaning a piece of cartilage is floating around. I played enough as a sophomore to letter as a center and linebacker but it was in my junior and senior years that I really progressed.

During my first two years Tommy Beene was the coach and he handled it all—football, basketball, everything. I don't remember whether he was a good coach but he was a good man and interested in the players. Then in my junior year we got a new head coach named Speedy Moffett. He was a short man with a deep, rumbling voice and his line coach was a bigger, rawboned guy named Mule Kayser. Both of them had played at

Texas Tech in the '30s under Pete Cawthon, who was legendary in the Southwest for his player discipline. They were tough disciplinarians, too, but they were good coaches and good men.

"One day," recalled Speedy Moffett, "we didn't have a very good workout so I had the team run up and down the stands awhile after practice. The next morning I had a call from one player's father.

"He said, 'Coach, it's a good thing I don't know where you live. I wanted to come after you with a shotgun last night when I saw the shape my boy was in when he got home. He was so worn out he nearly fell down in the front yard.'

"I said, 'Well, I'll give you my address so you'll know where to find me the next time.'

"At noon I ran into Bill Teaff. I said, 'Maybe you're mad at me, too. I worked the players awfully hard yesterday.' He said, 'Naw, pour it on 'em. It's good for 'em!'

"That shows you the type of background Grant had. He never minded hard work."

Snyder didn't win a district championship during Grant's years but to this day Speedy Moffett wishes he'd had more players like him on his first Tiger teams.

"He didn't have any speed but he had quickness and he had fine football instinct," Moffett said. "As a lineman he could get that explosion to make a block. As a linebacker he did a lot in his first few steps because he sensed where he should move. And he was a great contact player."

As a senior Grant made all-district and was co-captain. Didn't he ever clash with the coaches?

"Well, Grant was a good politician," Moffett said, grinning. "He may not have liked everything the coaches did but his attitude was 'If this is how you want it, that's great with me.' "

Mule Kayser recalled that Grant's protest took a subtle form.

"I insisted all the players call me Mr. Kayser," he said. "I told them when they were 21 they could call me Mule. 'You're in high school now and I'm your coach,' I said.

"One day I saw Grant stop by my car outside the locker room. It was covered with dust. With his finger he wrote in big letters on the trunk: 'Mule's Train'."

Mule Kayser was a tough son-of-a-gun. My senior year a few of us decided to cut classes on Friday afternoon before a game and relax at the picture show. We showed up at the field house about five o'clock to dress for the game and Coach Kayser was waiting for us. He knew we had cut class and he was somewhat hot.

There we were, almost grown men and Coach Kayser had us bending over while he whipped us with kindlin' wood. Later Coach Moffett told me he opened the door and saw me bent over and Coach Kayser blasting away and that kindlin' wood flying and bouncing off the walls. "I just turned around and went back to my car," he said. "I didn't know what in the world was going on."

Coach Moffett had some very successful teams later but when I was in high school we never had the winning tradition of a real West Texas power like Breckenridge or Odessa. Still, the involvement in football was the most important thing in my life. I also played basketball and once scored 19 points in a game but I mainly was a one-man demolition squad. I ran in a couple of track meets but only because Coach Kayser was also track coach and thought I should run the 880. They needed an eight-day clock to time me.

I was sort of nonchalant about my studies for awhile but as I got near graduation I worked hard in the classroom. I was student council president and I was determined to go to college. One summer of roughnecking in the oil field, heaving that steel around under a burning sun, convinced me I wanted enough education that I could choose what I wanted to do in life.

As a senior I received the Carl Herod Award which was voted annually to the outstanding football player. This was very special to me for an extra reason. Carl Herod was a dear friend, a retired coach who had become a successful business man in Snyder. He had originated that award in 1945 and I had dreamed of winning it since I was a boy.

> Carl Herod remembers fondly the day he met Grant.
>
> "I guess he was about ten but he wasn't the least bit shy," Herod said. "Grant's eyes were shining and he walked up and stuck out his hand. 'Mr. Herod,' he said, 'I've sure been looking forward to meeting you. Daddy told me that you've done a lot of coaching and there are some things I want to ask you.' When I got home I told my wife, 'I just met the most inspirational boy I've ever known.' "
>
> Herod also remembers not so fondly how Grant strayed briefly in the spring of his junior year.
>
> "There were a lot of new kids in school because of the oil boom and some of them were sorry students. I saw Grant over at Big Spring with them twice when he should have been in class. Next thing you knew it was time for final exams and Grant had fooled around so much he flunked algebra. That meant he would be ineligible for football and I told him to ask the teacher for a re-exam. 'It won't help,' he said. 'I've messed up too much. I'll just quit school and join the Marines.' But I talked him into getting the re-exam and then I worked with him day and night with the algebra book. He passed with no trouble and came straight to my house to tell me.
>
> " 'Carl,' he said, 'I want to make a covenant with you before God. I'll never again give anything less than my best effort.' "

Carl Herod had a profound influence on my life and so have a lot of other people. I'll always be thankful for them.

When I graduated from Snyder High School in June of 1951 I was excited about going to college but I really didn't know where it would be. By then my enthusiasm for coaching must have been apparent to everyone. In the class prophecy it was predicted that I some day would be head coach at the University of Texas.

Well, they only missed it 100 miles.

4.

From Walk-on to Winner

Each year when Grant Teaff tries to recruit the blue-chip high school athletes he still remembers how the other half lives. He was totally unsought when he graduated from Snyder High School in 1951 but still terribly anxious to play football for a college somewhere. Terribly anxious and determined.

Something which has really helped me in my coaching career is my willingness to give an opportunity to players who have displayed little talent but have a great yearning to play. They're walk-ons—unrecruited, non-scholarship types who simply want a chance to make your team. I believe in them because I was one myself.

Sam Harper, the starting tight end for our 1974 Southwest Conference champions at Baylor, was a walk-on and I've had plenty of others. Through the years I've probably had more little people play for me than most coaches. The only way Steve Beaird could measure 5-7 was by standing on his tip-toes but he was a tremendous tailback for us in '74, led the Southwest Conference in rushing, tandem offense, and scoring and wound up a pretty high draft choice with the pros. And Neal Jeffrey, who was perhaps the most inspirational quarterback in

Baylor history and good enough to make all-conference, was so slow for his position that it wasn't until he graduated that I revealed his 40-yard dash time was only 5.1 seconds. Heck, lots of linemen run faster than that.

Of course, if there's anyone who's an expert on not being very swift it's me. If a college scout ever bothered to look at me when I was in high school I'm sure he summed me up in four words: "Too light, too slow." I weighed 151 pounds and my speed was awful. That was before the practice of clocking players in the 40 but if I had been timed I'm sure it would have made Neal Jeffrey feel a little better.

But one coach, Max Bumgardner at San Angelo Junior College, gave me a chance and I've always remembered it. So any time a young man shows up with little to offer but desire I'll give him a chance. I miss on some of them and a lot of them have no business out on the field but I'll give everybody a chance because I got one.

When it was obvious no senior college was interested in me I asked my high school coach, Speedy Moffett, if he would help me get a tryout at a junior college. We wound up visiting San Angelo that spring and Coach Bumgardner simply told me I could report on September 1 for practice. He said if I made the team he'd give me a scholarship but he wasn't promising anything.

That was fine with me, so at the end of the summer I packed up my latest car, a 1937 deluxe Pontiac, and left Snyder for the 100-mile trip to San Angelo. I still tease my mother about how she stood on the front porch with tears streaming down her face because her baby boy was going off to college. But I was seventeen years old and excited about meeting the challenge of the new world, even if I didn't know a soul in San Angelo.

Once we got on the football field I was scared to death but I must have knocked people around pretty good. After a couple of days Coach Bumgardner called me in and said, "We're going to give you a scholarship." Funny thing was they didn't give me a new jersey. All of those already were assigned so I played the entire '51 season in an old faded jersey. But I started every game at linebacker and went on to start a total of fifty-one straight games throughout junior and senior college.

San Angelo was just a small school then, with no more than 800 students and a handful of buildings on its campus. We played our home games in Bobcat Stadium, the old high school field which seated about 6,000, but we played a strong, competitive schedule and had winning teams. Max Bumgardner was a good motivator and an unusual man.

He was still pretty young himself then, a guy who had finished playing college football after serving in World War II and became an all-Southwest Conference end at Texas when Bobby Layne was quarterback. He was a fire-and-brimstone type of coach, sometimes given to long orations in which he blistered the locker room with language equal to a longshoreman's. But he was full of paradoxes. He could be suave and debonair and charm the horns off a billy goat. Once he stood on a bench just before a game, raised his hand and led us in a long, drawn-out prayer. When he finished praying, he said, "Now let's go out and kill those blankety-blanks." We laughed about it but we always played well for him.

Once we were playing down in South Texas and we had a lousy first half. He didn't even come in the locker room at half-time. We sat around wondering where he was. Just as we were going out for the second half, he stuck his head in the door. "I just didn't want to be around guys who played that sorry," he told us. It was a psychological trick, of course, but it worked. We won in the second half.

I grew a lot after I turned eighteen and my second year at San Angelo I weighed 193. The games I remember best were our biggest trips, one to California to play Compton and another to Galveston to play Hinds, Mississippi, in the Oleander Bowl.

We rode the train to California and we all wore cowboy hats, figuring we should look the part of a team from Texas. That game left quite an impression because Compton had a fine team and we played before about 10,000 people, the biggest crowd I'd seen at that time. I was captain and I believe I showed pretty good leadership although I'm not sure now I'd approve of my behavior when I was called in by the officials to hear the options on a penalty.

We were standing near our bench and I heard voices screaming advice to me. We were losing and I already was pretty mad so I just turned and yelled, "I'm elected captain and I'll make the decision!"

Coming back everything was pretty relaxed on the train. Everybody was having fun but one guy got hold of some liquor and he really got stoned. When we pulled into the station at San Angelo there were a lot of people on that platform to greet us and we didn't want anyone to see him. A couple of us took the poor guy off the back side of the train and carried him behind some buildings until the crowd left. Then we got him in a car and took him to the dormitory. We didn't want him to be embarrassed but that wound up being a minor chapter in his life. He became an alcoholic and a few years later was killed in an auto accident.

We played in the Oleander Bowl on Thanksgiving Day 1952 and we started the game at 10:00 A.M. so it could be broadcast on radio. That was my only bowl experience until Baylor played Penn State in the 1975 Cotton Bowl and we lost that one, too. To make it worse, I was knocked colder than a wedge on the last play of the game and missed the big party they were throwing for us afterward. I had a slight concussion and no matter how I pleaded with the doctor I had to spend the night in the hospital.

After two seasons at San Angelo I had enjoyed some success and the senior college recruiters visited me then. I received scholarship offers from most of the smaller colleges in Texas and although no one from Texas A&M visited me I received word through Coach Bumgardner that if I wanted to transfer there I had a scholarship.

I didn't seriously consider A&M but if I had gone there I would have been on the team which Bear Bryant took to that historic fall training camp at Junction when he became head coach in '54. You still hear guys talk about how rough Bear's workouts were at Junction and how many players quit and went home. Gene Stallings once said, "We went to Junction in two buses and came back in one."

Of the larger schools, Texas Tech was the one that gave me a big rush. Tech wasn't yet in the Southwest Conference but was very ambitious and eager to build its football program. DeWitt Weaver, a real personable and live-wire guy who eventually led Tech into the Southwest Conference in 1956, had this old line coach named Wyatt Posey trying to recruit me. He was some kind of critter.

He visited me in my home in Snyder and really gave me a spiel about all the fun I'd have at Tech. He said there was a fabulous lake and the athletic department kept a yacht there which always was available to the players. Of course, I was raised in West Texas and I knew the only thing they had up at Lubbock was little ol' Buffalo Springs Lake which wasn't big enough to turn a yacht around on. The school probably kept a motor boat out there.

That was my first experience with a recruiter and I've always remembered it vividly. My own philosophy about recruiting goes back to that point. We may lose a lot of guys but I'll never tell one something that's not true.

I didn't go to Tech because that man told me something that wasn't right and I felt like if he were to be my coach the first thing I had to establish with him was some honesty. We couldn't have any kind of rapport without that.

There wasn't time to visit around a lot because I was going to transfer at mid-term in January of '53. I chose McMurry, a small Methodist college in Abilene, because that was the one place which offered a scholarship to my roommate and good friend, Jim Henderson. I spent three and a half years there because the eligibility rules then allowed me to play three seasons of senior college football after transferring from junior college. That was the beginning of a long and wonderful relationship with McMurry.

The people there were Christian men and women and I soon realized they loved McMurry. The school had known real tough times back in the '30s and couldn't pay the faculty money. All of the teachers just accepted script and exchanged it for goods at the stores. I had some teachers who once had worked at McMurry two or three years without receiving a penny because they loved the school and they were committed to Christian education.

McMurry, of course, was enjoying better times when I enrolled there. It never was a rich school but it is supported by the Methodist church and some new buildings were underway or being planned. There was a lovely chapel on the campus which all of the students attended daily. It was good exposure because I heard some fine speakers and good preachers there. Bible courses were required and although I didn't realize it then that knowledge would prove very beneficial to me through the years.

Wilford Moore was the head coach and I learned plenty from him. I had tremendous respect for him. He was not a great overall coach but he was a terrific offensive coach. I guess that was because he had played at Hardin-Simmons under Warren Woodson, who produced some of the most exciting offenses ever seen.

The greatest things I learned from Coach Moore were discipline, hard work and the vital role which respect plays in human relationships. Some players didn't like him and a lot of them feared him but everyone respected him.

He was fair and honest but mighty tough on us. He told me years later that his toughness went back to his days as a young coach right after World War II. He had a lot of veterans on his teams older than he was and he decided the only way to succeed was to be tougher than they were. This carried over into the '50s although he then was dealing with young players out of high school and junior college.

He'd have four-hour workouts and some grueling drills, like head-on tackling at 20 yards. He'd line men up every five yards down the field and you had to try to run over them while they tried to tackle you. We did some things that I didn't think were proper or right in coaching but some other traits of his coaching were important to me. And I never feared him.

We played 2-platoon football and he started me at offensive

tackle for our first game. I felt I was also the team's best line-backer and wanted to play both ways so after the game I talked to him about it. This was unheard of but I felt comfortable doing it because I believed what I was asking was right. He respected me enough to give me a chance at linebacker in the next game against Sul Ross. I had an outstanding game and the remainder of my three years at McMurry I played both offense and defense.

From that I learned the importance of communication. Young people need to know they can come and talk to you or ask questions without your being upset. My door is always open and a player can just walk in. If we're having a staff meeting my staff will get up and leave if the player wants to talk to me. All of my coaches take the same attitude. We're available and we'll listen.

My senior year in '55 Coach Moore resigned to enter private business and Doug Cox moved from Ballinger High School to become head coach. McMurry had one of the best records in Texas, 8–2, and won the Texas Conference title. By then I was getting very anxious to get a coaching job but I also made certain I had a diversified education.

I spent five years in college and the last couple of years I realized what a great opportunity I had, dug in and made top grades. Besides earning my bachelor of science degree in physical education, I also took a lot of business and history and government courses. If I hadn't gone into football coaching I might have tried law. I also was well on my way to earning a master's degree in administrative education when I finished my senior year in the spring of '56 so I decided I would return to McMurry in the summer of '57 and complete work on it.

I was fortunate to find a good assistant coaching job at a large high school, Tom S. Lubbock, where Wilford Moore had become head coach. I was excited and eager to start work, although at $3,500 I took a $500-a-year cut in salary from what I was making as a director for the Abilene television station, KIBC.

I first got into radio work in San Angelo, working as a disc jockey on a late-night program. I picked the records and I went for the placid music and some country-and-western. Johnnie Ray's first hit, "Cry" was popular then and I played it a lot. When I moved to Abilene I continued my radio work awhile, then moved into television when a new station opened. I started at the bottom, handling the camera, and worked up to director. By the time I graduated it had become a full-time job paying $4,000 a year. I enjoyed the work. It helped me learn to give directions, organize, and express myself clearly under pressure. But I gladly quit to move to Lubbock to coach and teach physical education.

I wasn't money-crazy. I had gone through college on scholarship and had made enough in various jobs to buy what I needed. I also had managed to save enough to buy a new car, a red-and-white Pontiac, thanks to a great summer job in Snyder. The city had built a big swimming pool in Towle Park, so after I took the courses to qualify as swimming instructor and lifeguard I went to work managing the pool for the park director, an old coach named Spider Dillon. He told me if I wanted to teach kids to swim I could keep all the fees. This proved quite profitable because hardly anyone in Snyder knew how to swim. There never had been a place to learn.

I would teach large classes all summer, charging $5 per lesson per child. Each child normally took six lessons so that was $30 a head. One summer I taught 600 to swim.

Spider Dillon is a good friend and he still likes to fuss at me about that. "I knew you were going to be a success," he told me once, "because there I was running the whole park and you were making five times as much money as I was."

5.

Something to Cheer About

Any young football coach quickly draws some scouting assignments when he joins a staff and it was no different with Grant Teaff on his first job at Tom S. Lubbock High School in the fall of '56. The scouting job he'll never forget, however, was purely voluntary.

I went to Texas Tech's first home game and sat in the stands, my binoculars fixed to my eyes. When I entered the stadium I was very interested in watching the game, but later I couldn't have given you any details of it. I couldn't even tell you whom Tech was playing.

What I vividly remembered was a good-looking blonde girl I saw on the sideline. She was leading yells for Tech at a very fast clip and with tremendous energy. I watched her throughout the game and I thought she was as beautiful as she was active. It was obvious to me that she liked something I liked: football. When I left the stadium I was really eager for Tech's next game.

I had dated a lot of girls during my college years but never had a serious romance. I had my football and my education to pursue and I didn't want to be that involved with anyone. When

I moved to Lubbock I was anxious to meet some girls when I ran into a friend from Snyder, Mary Alice Richardson, who was going to Tech. She told me she wanted to arrange a meeting with a girl she thought I would like very much. "Her name is Donell Phillips," she said, "and she's a cheerleader at Tech."

Immediately I thought of that girl in my binoculars. "She doesn't happen to be blonde, does she?" I asked. "Yes," she said, "she is blonde. She is Miss Lubbock and she's very beautiful."

I told her, "I think I know the one you're talking about and I would *lo-o-ove* to meet her." She said she'd try to make the arrangements.

Evidently she talked to Donell about it, too, because several nights later I walked into the women's dormitory at Tech to pick up a date and this beautiful bundle of energy bounded out from behind the switchboard at the reception desk. She literally prissed up to me and asked, "Aren't you Grant Teaff?"

My cleverness at that moment astounded me. "Well, yes I am," I said. "Well," she said, "I'm Donell Phillips."

"I'm happy to know you," I said, hoping my face didn't tell her right then just how happy I really was. I was trying to act like a big shot and not be too impressed. But I was deeply impressed. And I think she was, too.

All of these guys were hurrying in, calling for girls and leaving on their dates and we stood there looking at each other. "Well," I said, "how about having a Coke?" She said, "You have a date, don't you?" "Yes," I told her. "I mean tomorrow." She gave me a big smile.

I didn't think a lot about the girl I was with that night. When I brought my date back to the dorm I craned my neck, trying to get another glimpse of Donell. I didn't see her but I hurried back to my apartment and called her to confirm our Coke date for the next day. I could hardly wait to pick her up.

I guess you read in romantic books about love at first sight. I wasn't sure about that, but I knew I felt a deep attraction—and not only to her beauty. There was something about her that was tremendously appealing. She had an air of confidence and she was very articulate. It was fun to be with her.

I asked her for a full-fledged date that evening. We went to the picture show but don't ask me the title or what it was about. It was like that first Tech football game: I was thrilled to be there but I didn't know what I was watching. I do remember that I very boldly held her hand. And that was the beginning of one of the most beautiful parts of my life: a continuing, growing relationship with Donell.

We fell deeply in love and it wasn't long before my roommate, another young coach named Ronald Robbins, knew he'd have to find someone else to share that apartment. Donell had only one more semester left before graduation so we decided to get married as quickly as possible.

> Grant and Donell were a couple with a great deal in common. They were children of the '30s, born during hard times and raised in modest circumstances but both were possessed with unusual ambition.
>
> Donell was born in Munday, "a sandy little place near Wichita Falls," and lived there until she was in the eighth grade. Then her father, weary of the meager living they made from their cotton farm, sold everything they owned and moved the family to Plainview, fifty miles north of Lubbock. They had irrigation there and farming was very successful until he became ill her senior year in high school. They sold their farm and some years later invested in a women's clothing store in Plainview. For a time Donell and Grant held an interest in the store. Donell gained valuable experience helping her mother at seasonal markets. A woman of varied talents and interests, she received a degree in business administration from Texas Tech although she first wanted to study medicine when she entered college. And she always had loved sports.
>
> "I had been a cheerleader as long as I could remember," Donell said. "This was conducive to being a coach's wife. I was interested in many of the same things he was. We had a common ground.

"Grant struck me as someone who really knew what he wanted to do in life. He always has been a very confident individual who understood where he wanted to go and what he wanted to be. I liked this about him."

We were married and moved into a small apartment. Ironically, it was located on Baylor Street in Lubbock. It really was small—a tiny kitchen and living room-dining room combination with a tiny bedroom and adjoining bath. It was a very good place to start our married life. You could really feel togetherness in a place like that.

Meanwhile, my first year in coaching and teaching was eventful. As a coach, I learned a lot about working with young players. As a teacher, I learned even more about understanding people.

When we opened workouts at Lubbock High that fall I first worked with the B team but soon my old college coach, Wilford Moore, moved me up to work with the varsity defense. We had one young man who really caught my eye. His name was E.J. Holub and I never had seen anyone who could hit a 7-man sled by himself and drive it back like he could. He was a tremendous hitter!

Holub later became an all-American linebacker and center at Texas Tech and went on to become all-pro for the Dallas Texans and Kansas City Chiefs. Unfortunately he didn't play for us his senior year. Coach Moore, of course, was a very tough disciplinarian and was trying hard to establish a winning program. E.J. had some disagreement with him over his participation in track the previous spring and he dropped out of football that fall.

I was fresh out of college and so enthusiastic about my work on the field that one day I asked Coach Moore for permission to put on a headgear and shoulder pads and demonstrate. I felt like a hoss, because I could really knock those young guys around. That was the first and last time I demonstrated with pads on a football field. After about 30 minutes I realized I wasn't in as good condition as I once was although I had finished college football only a year before. I was really dragging when that afternoon ended. I decided to become a coach who could teach them how to do it without actually showing them how in full pads.

As a physical education teacher, I could have made good use of the advice Tommy Ellis later gave me when I returned to McMurry as an assistant coach on his staff. "Never make a snap judgment about a player," he said. I learned during my first semester as a teacher that also should be applied to any student.

I hadn't dealt with teen-agers before. In college my practice teaching had been in elementary schools. When I went to Lubbock High I wanted to apply all my tremendous knowledge as a football player to my P.E. classes.

I think I was a good P.E. teacher, one with real interest in the physical development of all young people. We played one game called eat-'em-up-soccer—soccer played on a basketball court with a mat behind the goalpost for the scoring zone. I liked it because it was a contact sport. The boys got out there in their shorts and gym shoes and they had to be pretty tough to play it. I liked to see an aggressive young person and it was good conditioning because they had to keep moving all the time.

There was one young man who had been rather reserved in all the activities. He was frail, about 5–9 or 5–10 and weighed only 125 pounds or so, but he didn't look sickly. When we got into eat-'em-up soccer he always got at a far corner of the gym and avoided contact.

I spoke to him rather harshly, telling him to get out and mix it up. He'd get out awhile, then I'd look again and he'd be back against the wall. I really didn't know what to do with him. He kind of repulsed me because he wouldn't hit. At the end of the semester I gave him a low grade because he didn't participate.

He came by to see me. He looked at me and said, "Mister Teaff, you don't like me."

That kind of stunned me, because deep inside me the guilt was there. I didn't like him because he was a non-hitter, but I lied to him. "Of course, I like you," I told him. "I like you just as much as anyone in this class." He saw through me. "No, sir, you don't like me," he said. "I can tell."

About two weeks later I was in the gym when one of the classroom teachers sent a girl to find me, saying she needed help immediately. I sprinted to her room and found my reluctant soccer player on the floor. He was in an epileptic seizure. He had swallowed his tongue and his face was growing discolored.

I quickly started to work on him, got his mouth open and got him to breathing properly. Suddenly a cold chill went up my spine as I looked at that boy I had treated so harshly.

We contacted his mother, then put him on a couch to rest before she took him home. When she arrived I walked out to the car with him.

"Why didn't you tell me you were an epileptic?" I asked him. "Why didn't you ask for special P.E.?"

He said, "Mister Teaff, I just wanted to be a part of everything but I was afraid if I got out on the floor and got hit that I might have a seizure. And it is so embarrassing when I do."

That taught me a tremendous lesson. I don't know where that young man is today but I know I've never looked at people the same since that day. I understand each individual has problems unique to himself and he knows what they are. If I am to be a leader of young men then it is my responsibility to know and understand the things in their lives that are important to them. Until you do, you never can hope to do your job.

6.
The Right Track

When they married, Grant and Donell Teaff set
their career goals for the next ten years. They divided them into three-year segments: first as a small
college assistant coach, next small college head coach
and then major college assistant coach. In the tenth
year, they felt he should be starting three years as a
head coach at a fairly large school such as a state
college. All of this, they believed, could carry them
to the ultimate goal: head coach at a Southwest Conference school.

Several months later in the spring of 1957 they
were delighted to see the first phase of their goals
materialize on schedule. They already had planned to
spend that summer in Abilene while Grant finished
work on a master's degree in administrative education
at his alma mater, McMurry College, and now Mc-
Murry was offering them an opportunity to stay.
Tommy Ellis, the head football coach, had an opening on his staff and wanted Grant to fill it. There was
one hitch. He would have to double as track and field
coach.

To say that I had reservations about coaching track is an

71

understatement. I knew nothing about that sport. I thought the track was something that held the football field together. Oh, I had run a little once but only because Mule Kayser, my line coach at Snyder High, insisted on it.

He also was track coach and he decided all the football players would be on the team. He looked at different guys and assigned an event. He just told me, "You're going to be a half-miler."

Naturally I didn't know how to run a half-mile. My first race was in a little county meet and when the starter fired that gun I did the only thing I knew to do, took off as hard as I could go. I was running wide open while other runners were pacing themselves but I didn't realize how far we would be running. On the back side of the track I thought maybe it was almost over but we just kept running. After one lap, 440 yards, I was leading by maybe a hundred yards, and looking for the finish line. Then I saw a horrible sight. The officials were waving me on.

I really don't know how I made it around the track again. I had the blind staggers and everyone passed me. Finally I crossed the finish line, weaved over to the stands, crawled up a couple of steps and flopped on my face. Mule Kayser stood there shaking his head. He decided I needed more experience.

Our next meet was in Roscoe and I showed my ingenuity. The track on the far side went behind the stands so on the first lap I stopped there, waited until the other runners came around again and rejoined them. I finished pretty good but Coach Kayser happend to be watching me. After he chastised me, we decided the half-mile wasn't my thing. End of track career.

Now I was being asked to coach a *college* track team! I didn't want to look foolish and I didn't want to do a sorry job and I definitely wanted to be a part of the McMurry football staff. So I decided I'd learn everything I could about track and do the best I possibly could.

The McMurry track program wasn't an overwhelming thing when I took over. The city of Abilene was tremendously track-conscious and Abilene Christian College was a national power with such stars as Olympic sprint champion Bobby Morrow. But the fever hadn't reached our campus. I had one scholarship, one stopwatch, and one NCAA track and field guide. I read that guide religiously, trying to absorb every detail about every event. And Carl Herod, my great old friend in Snyder, gave me a set of books he had saved from a clinic conducted by Dean Cromwell, the famous coach at the University of Southern California. I learned a lot about various events from those books. An excellent section on the long jump showed the proper technique and form when you rapidly flipped pages of pictures of an athlete making his jump from start to finish.

These proved very valuable to a guy who had to be the greenest track coach a college ever had. I had no idea how good my teams would be but I knew I wouldn't kiss them off just because my lifetime ambition was in football.

Once that problem was resolved the move to Abilene really became exciting. Donell was expecting our first child and I was anxious to make some money while I completed work on my master's so I resumed my work as a director at the television station and also taught swimming lessons. Since Donell still had a few days left at Texas Tech and also wanted to visit her mother in Plainview, she kept our car while I loaded an old pick-up truck I had gotten from my dad and started the move from Lubbock to Abilene.

All our worldly goods consisted of our clothes and a set of pots and pans, souvenirs of my career selling Wearever products while I was in college. Joe Bill Fox, one of my closest friends and teammates, and I decided we would make a fortune selling that stuff so we went to an organizational sales meeting. It was one of the first real pep rallies I ever attended.

One thing they said really has carried over with me in recruiting: "If you make twenty calls you're definitely going to make one sale." So I've never been shy about approaching young men to come to my school. I figured if I contacted enough good ones and presented my case in a proper manner, I would have the opportunity to coach my share of them. It's pretty well worked that way through the years and I can credit that theory to Wearever.

That theory and that set of pots and pans were about all I ever got out of Wearever, though. We had to set up home demonstrations and Joe Bill and I were lousy cooks. So I gave my set to Donell and lovingly loaded them up for the trip south to Abilene.

I got brave and scouted around for a place to live and finally found a duplex on Peach Street, which struck me as an appropriate name. I thought the place was super and worked hard to have it ready when Donell arrived. I was real disappointed when she walked in and started crying.

I thought she didn't like it but later I learned she did. It was just that the trip had been hard on her, being pregnant and moving away from her mother. When she walked in the finality of being Mrs. Teaff was upon her. We had moved to another part of the state and she knew no one but me. It never occurred to me it was such a drastic change. Abilene was my old haunt and I knew everyone.

That summer was one of tremendous transition for us. On August 4 our first daughter, Tammy, was born and by then we were preparing to move into our third home in Abilene. After a few weeks in the duplex we accepted an offer of a house which was rent-free as long as I did the yard work. Then came the opportunity to take an apartment in the athletic dorm, where I would serve as manager and counselor in addition to my coaching duties and teaching physical education.

Hunt Hall had been built in the late '20s or early '30s, shortly after McMurry was founded in Abilene, and I remembered it as a dilapidated mess. It was the same big old house I had moved into when I transferred from San Angelo in 1953. I sat on my bed then looking at that terrible room with its old high ceilings, Army bunks and a sink with a light bulb over it and asking myself, "What in the world am I doing at McMurry?" I had the urge to leave but I stayed and came to love that college. I knew that the rooms in which you lived were not as important as the people around you and the attitude you had about being there.

But when Donell and I moved into the dorm it was freshly painted. Tommy Ellis and I had worked very hard for a couple of weeks to get it in shape but it still wasn't much to bring a young wife and mother into. But we enjoyed fixing up that apartment. It had an entrance from the lobby, a little fenced area around the back door, and great neighbors. We had a fine relationship with all the young men in the dorm—about ninety scholarship athletes—and they adored having a brand new baby in the house.

My salary that first year at McMurry was $4,200, which really amounted to a lot more since we had no rent or utility bills to pay and ate most of our meals free in the campus cafeteria. We also lived there my second year on the staff, when I was raised to $4,600. By my third year I was making $6,000 and we bought a new home on Woodard Street. We had been able to build a nice savings account because of the minimal expenses of dorm living and the fact that Donell went to work as a private secretary for General Electric when Tammy was six months old. I was concerned about her working when Tammy was so young but we had a wonderful lady keeping Tammy while she was away and we were anxious to have our own home. At that time I guess we put more money in the bank than we ever have, allowing us to build a solid financial base in our early years of marriage.

The dorm life was good because I was about the same age as the athletes living there and everyone felt comfortable. It was important for them to know I was in a position of authority, but that carried over naturally enough from the football field. Of course, no one ever saw a "dorm mother" as beautiful as Donell. She was super.

We introduced some changes which some people may have thought were out of line, but they improved life in the dorm. On Saturday night we served Coke and punch and invited the guys to bring their dates to the dorm. We played records and they danced and everyone had a great time. I knew from my college experience they didn't have any money and we wanted to provide some entertainment.

The biggest problem in dorm behavior was somebody rolling a 16-pound shot from one end of the hall to the other over our apartment. That stopped the moment I appeared upstairs and mentioned it. The boys were courteous to Donell and really very concerned about their noise because of Tammy. Those two years in that dorm were one of the great experiences of my coaching career because I learned a lot about dealing with young men.

Meanwhile, my experiences in coaching were valuable in setting my philosophy for head coaching. I'm a great observer of people and an emulator when the things they do and say are good. The value of a good rapport with the young people you work with is something I learned very early.

The McMurry squad included the Baldwin brothers, Charlie and Jimmy, two of the toughest guys you'll ever meet. Seymour was their hometown and people there rolled their eyes when you mentioned their names. Both went on to become fine coaches and good friends but when I started coaching there they were known as rough customers. Still they were very warm and responsive to a young coach.

One day we were working hard on some line drills. I stopped for a moment to let the players catch their breath while I mentioned something I considered important. It was during two-a-days and just to break the monotony I nudged a cigarette butt out of the grass with my toe and kicked it. Charlie Baldwin was standing there so I said, "Charlie, you dropped something."

Everybody laughed and we quickly moved back into our drill. I never saw Charlie so intense about anything as he was then. Afterward, when we were walking off the field, he put his arm around my shoulder.

"Listen," he said, "I don't know how you found out I was smoking but if you won't tell Coach Ellis I promise you I won't ever do it again."

As sternly as I could, I said, "All right, Charlie. If you promise me you'll give it up I won't say a word." He walked away feeling very relieved and very happy that I would not break his confidence.

The spring always was extremely busy because I devoted a lot of time to coaching track and we also had football practice, but I loved it. I was learning more about track all the time and I was proud to see the team improving.

We became highly competitive among the Texas college division teams and then we began to develop a national reputation. Perhaps my original greenness worked in my favor, because I never insisted that only polished athletes report to my track team.

In track recruiting I learned you could search out undeveloped talent or talent that had yet to reach its full potential, and come up with some outstanding athletes. I applied this to football, too, and it also helped us.

The major colleges would pretty well clean out the state as far as the recognized athletes were concerned. I certainly wasn't going to land any of the blue-chippers. I had to recruit potential and develop it. That was the case with Bill Miller, a skinny little fellow from Winters. He had tremendous spring in his legs, good speed and that quality I watch for as much as anything, the ability to compete. He became one of the best athletes in Texas.

He was the first Texan to long jump over 26 feet, his career best being 26-6¾, and he won national titles. He was a great sprinter, ran on our sprint relay team and became an outstanding triple jumper. He participated overseas and in 1964 he missed qualifying for the U.S. Olympic team in the long jump by a half inch.

John Dale Lewis, another little-known athlete from Coleman, became a 9.3 sprinter and he and Bill gave us the nucleus for some fine relay teams in the early '60s. He had those same traits —great intensity and competitiveness.

When I started my track recruiting I wove my way through West Texas and then as we improved and traveled more widely, I did some recruiting nationwide. I learned that the more you moved around, the more people you met and the more tips you heard on good but unheralded prospects. I even recruited some foreign athletes. Ian Studd was a fine miler and 2-miler from New Zealand and Jasim Karasha, a 440 man, came from Baghdad. And in the mid-60s I had a national champion 440 intermediate hurdler, David Bonds, and another great long jumper in Freddie Fox, who became the second Texan to jump past 26 feet. That old picture book Carl Herod gave me sure did wonders for my reputation as a long jump coach.

What had started as a strange, secondary job when I joined

the McMurry staff in 1957 became an important part of my life. When I was promoted to head football coach in 1960 I could have dropped the track coaching but by then I was so involved with the sport and the athletes that I decided to keep it and work that much harder.

We ran that track program, including the recruiting, on a shoestring budget and still wound up with one of the best small college programs in the country. Without question the experience I had recruiting track people applied to my philosophy in recruiting football players. I look for the same characteristics. And when I became head football coach I was filled with confidence because of my success as a track coach. I knew if I could go into that job with no experience and be successful, I surely could succeed in football, where I felt I had some expertise.

> "I don't remember any time Grant felt frustration or felt he was ill-prepared for the job in those first years," Donell recalled. "If he didn't know, he never was bashful about asking someone for help, or getting a book and reading it.
> "It amazed me how he was able to do so well and be so knowledgeable. It's always seemed to me a coach should be an assistant for a long period but in observing Grant I realized he had the ability to be a head coach almost immediately. He had knowledge or knew where to get it. He constantly absorbed from everyone around him."

McMurry had a good football program under Tommy Ellis and the best year was 8–2 in 1959. A few weeks later he accepted an assistant's job under Jim Myers at Texas A&M and on Jan. 23, 1960, little more than two months past my 26th birthday, I was named head coach at McMurry. Donell and I were thrilled and delighted. We were expecting our second child, Tracy, who arrived on April 12; we were settled in our new home, and we were right on schedule with our goals, moving into a small college head coaching job in our fourth year.

As a player my coaches always stressed the importance of conditioning and that carried over in my coaching career. So I started a weight training program at McMurry, one of the first in the country, and we did it with homemade equipment.

My staff and I took cans from the cafeteria, filled them with wet concrete, sank iron poles in them and let them dry. Then we used them as barbells. Later we were able to buy some equipment from a weight studio in Abilene and converted a barracks to a weight room by knocking out the inside walls. We were quick to get into isometrics and we used overhead monkey bars every day. I believed we could eliminate shoulder injuries by using them and we did.

I also believed in the value of a running harness, rigged up by attaching ropes to one, two or three towers. This caused the athlete wearing it to gain the proper body lean and leg drive. John Dale Lewis, the sprinter, also became a powerful running back by using it.

These theories of development, of course, stemmed from the fact that I knew a small school like McMurry was going to recruit young athletes who were under-developed. These methods helped them reach their potential. We got a lot of football players into developmental running through our track program: running in place, proper placing of the hands and coordination with the feet, lifting the knees, all of the things important to running. We found that 90 percent of the guys coming out of high school didn't know how to run so we spent a lot of time teaching them how.

When I moved to Texas Tech, Coach J T King asked me to put in this program. I kept statistics on it the three years I was there and we could see that about 90 percent of the players improved their 40-yard dash time from one to three tenths of a second. Later when I moved to Angelo State and Baylor I used this program and saw positive results. I believe one reason for our early success at Baylor was the developmental running program we introduced the first spring, and it can be traced to that first experience at McMurry.

By the spring of '63 I felt great about the entire program. In football, after a rebuilding year in '60, McMurry had two winning seasons and the outlook was bright. And the track program really was glowing. It looked like a real high point in my career and, although we still had goals which called for me to move on, we weren't pushing it. The track job opened at Baylor when Jack Patterson, who had brought the school its first three championships in a four-year period, quit to move to the University of Texas. I talked about the job with John Bridgers, the athletic director and head football coach, but I was interested in a dual situation involving an assistant's job in football. Coach Bridgers said they planned to hire strictly a track coach, which they soon did with Clyde Hart. I thought I could have done well in both jobs for Baylor then but I wasn't shaken up because it didn't work out.

What did shake me up was picking up a newspaper while I was attending the Texas Coaching School in Houston that August and reading that McMurry was dropping the athletic scholarship program to ease its financial burden. That was the first word I had of such a move and I was stunned. It so limited the future for all of our sports that we knew it would be almost impossible to recruit new athletes and that those already at McMurry likely would decide to transfer to schools with full-fledged programs.

A lot of them did leave and I couldn't blame them. Frankly, I thought about leaving, too. I took time to weigh everything, though. Every impulse, every bit of advice was to get out. I spent a great deal of time praying that I would go the way God wanted me to go. Finally I talked to my pastor at Southwest Park Baptist Church, Brother Earl Sherman. "Just be assured," he told me, "that God has a special place for you."

I thought about that and how much I loved McMurry and I decided to stay and fight to reestablish our athletic program. Donell, who always has that loving ability to gently nudge me when I get off-course, understood my commitment and we settled down to revise our goals. At a time when we once had planned to launch our third three-year period in an assistant's job at a major school, instead we were staying with a little school that was down and out. And we had no assurance that my coaching career wouldn't wind up the same way. All we had was that commitment and our belief that God would guide us.

Ultimately the program was reestablished because I appealed to the school administration and the board of trustees to consider the great human value of a solid athletic program. There were more than 125 McMurry graduates coaching in Texas and I stressed the value of influencing athletes who would go into coaching. This was not something which could be measured in dollars and cents and I was thankful the school decided it was worth it.

After two and a half years, by the end of 1965, we finally won the battle and everything was sound again. McMurry had joined the Lone Star Conference and started giving 55 full scholarships. My record had deteriorated but the overall value of this achievement made it worthwhile. And I found I had grown in many ways, not only in athletics but with my children and Donell and in my relationship with God. But it all emerged from a terribly difficult period in the last few months of '63 when we were confronted with one shock after another. After losing the scholarship program, there was the plane crash in Louisiana which we miraculously survived, a losing season, and the tragedy of President Kennedy's assassination.

Through my six years as McMurry's head football coach I could also look back on some big moments on the field. I was particularly proud of our achievements against Abilene's two other church-supported schools, Hardin-Simmons and ACC.

Hardin-Simmons, a Baptist school widely known for playing major colleges and which once had Sammy Baugh as coach, had never played McMurry, the little old Methodist school, until I took over. We beat them three straight years during which time they had three different coaches. Then their administration decided to drop football and I felt very bad about it. Football is a great asset to a school and I'm afraid our three victories over them probably influenced their decision.

Our crosstown rivalry with ACC, the Church of Christ college, was a continuing thing and highly competitive. The game unofficially decided who was the city champion of Abilene. My first year as head coach ACC beat us 26–0. I showed that game film at least a hundred times before the next season's game. I promised the players if they beat ACC we would burn the film. Maybe that helped, because we won a real thriller, 33–28. Then ACC won three straight so by '65 we had a lot to overcome.

We had no business beating ACC that year. They had a big fullback, Mike Love, who could have played for any Southwest Conference school. They had outstanding tackles and a fine overall team. But I just felt we could beat them and I started my psychological build-up almost two weeks in advance. We hadn't beaten ACC in three years and I wanted to build on that aspect.

Since we were the McMurry College Indians we threw some supposedly Indian names around although I never was certain they were. We had a chant we used at homecoming, "Allah Cumba," and then we beat a drum a lot. Coaches who played us at homecoming told me the most feared sound around Mc-Murry was the beat of that drum. Our students would beat it all night long and right up until kickoff. It really had a hypnotic effect. We won a great number of homecoming games and I believe that was a factor.

We said "Allah Cumba" meant "Give us Victory" and I kept telling the players before the ACC game we wanted Cumba, meaning victory, on our fourth try and how that chant always helped us at homecoming. Meanwhile, I secretly ordered some new jerseys for the game. Each had the player's name on the back and on the front was "Cumba 4."

A couple of days before the game I leaked the word to the press about our special campaign, going after victory on the fourth try, but made no mention of the jerseys. The night of the game we warmed up in our old jerseys but while the players were on the field a manager hung a new one in each locker so each player would see them when they came in just before the game. First they would see their names on the back, then take them off the hook and see "Cumba 4."

When our players saw those jerseys their feet hardly touched the floor. I told them that all night the ACC players would be looking right at that Cumba 4, knowing that we were going to have victory on the fourth try. Throughout the game they heard our students chanting "Cumba 4! Cumba 4!" At halftime we were playing to the very best of our ability. I told the players if they won, those special jerseys would be theirs forever. They got even higher.

Although ACC was talented and much bigger we did win 9–8. We won only four games that year but that one night made my final season at McMurry much sweeter.

Besides all the emotional moments in my career there we had an experience with Tracy as a baby which we'll never forget. In the summer of '61 when she was 15 months old we were driving back to Abilene after visiting in Plainview and Snyder when we noticed Tracy couldn't sit up on her pallet in the back of our station wagon. We tried to right her but her head kept pulling back and she felt clammy. This really scared us and as soon as we reached Abilene we took her to our pediatrician, Dr. Jake Barron.

He looked at Tracy and immediately called the hospital. He calmly told us to check her in for some tests but we knew he was quite concerned. After a while Dr. Barron came to the waiting room and said, "Sit down. I want to tell you something.

"It looks like Tracy has spinal meningitis," he told us. I can't describe the shock we felt.

He said there was going to be a spinal tap, a very painful thing. I sat through that and it just tore my insides out to watch them do that to a little baby.

Donell and I went in a room and knelt to pray. I've never prayed harder in my life nor has Donell. We already had committed ours to be a Christian family when we married but we renewed that commitment. Maybe we had drifted away. I don't know. We made some commitments which changed both of our lives. Donell has been a strength to me because of those commitments, which she has stuck with totally.

We told God we probably had not been the total Christian family we should have been, but we vowed to renew our commitment as we prayed for Tracy's life.

I don't know how long we prayed. There really wasn't anything else we could do. Finally, when all the tests were finished, Dr. Barron was in utter amazement. Every test was negative.

I'm not saying Tracy had spinal meningitis and God healed her. But I do know that very sound medical people said she had spinal meningitis and she had the symptoms. In a couple of days she was all right and never had another problem. We are just thankful to God for answering our prayers to spare her.

That commitment kept us tied directly to the church and helped us to grow. We believe in the unity of the family and church. We've taught Sunday school since the early days of our marriage, working mostly with high school and college ages, young married couples, and career types. After that ordeal with Tracy and after the plane crash, I became a Baptist deacon in December of '63. And through it all Donell has been the beautiful influence in my life and those of our three daughters.

Our third daughter, Layne, also was born in Abilene. It was Saturday, September 11, 1965, we were opening the season against Angelo State that night and naturally I was hoping for a boy.

I think every man has that innate desire for a reproduction of himself. I had all those aspirations through the years for Grant Garland Teaff Jr. We also had some other boys' names we liked. Todd was a special favorite. We always liked the double T's in our children's names. In fact, all our girls have the initials TLT—Tamera Lea Teaff, Teresa Lynn Teaff and Terri Layne Teaff. We decided to call the last one Layne, however, because we were starting to stutter with all those T-T's.

The same doctor, Lee Rode, delivered all three babies and just as Donell went into the delivery room before Layne was born he told me he was sure from the heartbeat that this baby was a boy. The nurse believed it, too. She kept telling me, "It's a boy! It's a boy!"

I called Dr. Rode aside. "You say that's a boy," I told him, "but how strongly do you believe that's a boy?" He said, "I've listened to a lot of babies' heartbeats. I can tell that's a boy."

"Tell you what I'll do," I said. "If it is a boy, I'll pay you double. If it's another girl, then I get her free." "Naw," he said, "I don't want to do that."

So they wheeled Donell into the delivery room and *that boy* turned out to be another precious little girl. That night we defeated Angelo State and the players gave Layne the game ball. On Sunday morning I carried it to the hospital and held it up while I looked at her through the window of the newborn nursery. That football was bigger than she was.

In the summer of '66 I was approaching my seventh year as McMurry's head coach, a job I already had held twice as long as our original goals called for. There had been earlier opportunities for assistant's jobs at Southwest Conference schools, once at SMU and another time at A&M, but I had doubts about where such moves could take me. History indicated that Southwest Conference assistants very rarely moved up to the head coaching job at their schools.

But that summer I participated in a clinic at Dallas with J T King of Texas Tech and we got along extremely well. Later he offered me an assistant's job and in August I decided to take it.

It was a very tough decision, leaving McMurry after spending so many years of our lives there, but this wasn't just another assistant's job. I would also be recruiting director and we would be at Texas Tech, where Donell and I had especially hoped some day I would become head coach.

So we finally said goodbye to McMurry. We all broke down and cried at the parting. I believe you can see why.

7.

Fresh Inspiration

Donell Teaff remembered the three football seasons at Texas Tech as "an interim time in our life. Moving into an assistant coach's job was very difficult for Grant because he is very much his own man. He's much more a leader than a follower, and always has been, but he knew he needed the experience of working on the Tech staff. I admired him because he wanted to broaden his horizons."

From a family standpoint, that period in 1966-68 was very satisfying. Everyone enjoyed life in Lubbock. Particularly Donell, who found special enjoyment in returning to her alma mater as the wife of a coach. And the fact that Grant left McMurry for Tech with the outlook he did proved a great plus for the man who hired him. J T King sensed that a coach of Grant's unusual background and ability could broaden the horizons for the entire Red Raider program.

King at the time was a veteran football man in his 50's who, in contrast to the youthful Teaff, had served most of his career as a college assistant before becoming a head coach. He had coached at Texas and

A&M before joining DeWitt Weaver's staff at Tech in 1958. In '61 he was promoted to head coach, an uncommon move in the Southwest Conference where the recent history has been one of hiring a head coach from another school. A guard at Texas in the mid-30s, King had something in common with Grant. That was a nose for football, and not just because each had his broken a few times. King appreciated Grant's football ability but even more he admired his unusual personal quality.

"The main thing I remember Grant for was his complete confidence in what he was doing, be it coaching, recruiting or just talking to people," King said. "He was always cool, always in control of the situation."

Or as John Scovell, a star Tech quarterback of that era, noted, "He just kinda had it all together."

J T King was a good man to work for because he understood my goals and he wanted to help me pursue them while also letting me handle some important jobs for him. We developed a fine rapport and a great mutual respect which I'll always treasure.

When Jake hired me my primary coaching duty was to be working with the offensive ends but I wanted more responsibility so he quickly made me recruiting coordinator. Since I've always enjoyed meeting people and speaking he soon had me working heavily in a public relations capacity, attending banquets and other meetings and appearing frequently on his TV show. And he assigned me two specific jobs which represented the greatest problems in Tech's history: recruiting in West Texas and scouting the University of Texas.

When Tech gained membership in the Southwest Conference in 1956 there was great excitement about the rich recruiting potential in West Texas. This was Tech's backyard and many people assumed the school now would become the most attractive of all the major colleges which recruited in that area. But that was not the case. While Tech had become a successful recruiter in major metropolitan areas in other parts of the state like Houston, Dallas and Fort Worth, it consistently failed to recruit well in West Texas.

It could be traced to the fact that Tech simply had a poor image in its own section of Texas. This was an old problem, one resulting from mistakes made by an earlier administration before Tech entered the conference. West Texas basically is composed of small towns, ones where everybody knows everybody else and what those people saw of some Tech coaches then had left the impression that they were big-timers not interested in developing ties as good neighbors. They didn't spend the time making friends with the high school coaches and athletes that they should have. This created barriers for Tech and years later I took on the job of tearing down those barriers.

It was tough. It took a long time to change some attitudes about Tech but gradually the doors began to open and everything became more comfortable. I traveled the West Texas territory constantly, speaking and visiting, developing a personal interest in those towns, their schools, their athletes and coaches. Finally we had an atmosphere in which Tech could become a positive force.

After a couple of years Tech began to score heavily in West Texas recruiting. Fine prospects were everywhere once you knew how to find them and had the contacts to reach them. I'll never forget how surprised Coach King was when I told him I wanted to give full scholarships to two players from Bronte. That's a little town near San Angelo, a Class B school, and you normally don't find a player at a Class B school who can start for a Southwest Conference team. Now I was telling him I had found two at one school. He accepted my judgment, however, and those players wound up making all-conference, Doug McCutcheon as a running back and Davis Corley as a defensive end. A number of other all-conference players came from my West Texas recruits. Some of them were Larry Molinaire, a linebacker from Midland; Mark Dove, a defensive back from San Angelo; and Jerry Watson, a safety from Ranger who also made all-America.

It was a major breakthrough for Tech and naturally I was

proud to be involved in it, just as I was with the one Tech scored on the field against Texas.

Since entering the conference football race in 1960 Tech had lost seven straight times to the Longhorns, usually by lopsided scores. Texas traditionally has fine teams under Darrell Royal but the way they totally dominated this rivalry was embarrassing to everyone at Tech. They always played in September, the first conference game for both schools, and the experience repeatedly left Tech in a hole. So in '67 Jake told me I would be in charge of preparations for the Texas game.

I went to Los Angeles and scouted Texas in its opener against Southern California. Texas lost 17–13 but that was a fine USC team featuring a new running back named O. J. Simpson. Those Longhorns were impressive, but I felt good about Tech's chances as I flew back to Lubbock.

When I got home I told Donell, "We can beat Texas." Naturally, she wanted to know why.

"I think this is all psychological with Tech," I said. "There's a mental block about Texas. This Tech team is sound. We have good players and the coaches know their business. If we'll just close the door on the past, start this week with a positive attitude and do our work, we can go to Austin next Saturday night and win."

Donell listened with interest. She knew me and my outlook better than anyone. But on Monday Jake asked me to join him at the weekly boosters' luncheon sponsored by the Red Raider Club at a downtown hotel. I gave my scouting report on Texas and then told them the same thing I had told Donell. The audience was stunned and Jake almost fell out of his chair. My statement really put him on the spot.

"Well," he said when he rose to speak, "I'm glad Grant believes that because if we don't beat Texas, he's fired!"

Fortunately, I never had to learn whether Jake was kidding. A great enthusiasm and confidence permeated the Tech players and coaches that week. Jake put together a great game plan and that Saturday night the team took the field in Memorial Stadium at Austin and executed it with the same poise they might have displayed against any other opponent. Tech kicked the old Texas hex by winning 19–13 and the next year at Lubbock proved it was no fluke by winning again 31–22.

After we won in Austin the team plane couldn't land at the Lubbock airport because the runway was swarming with 10,000 Tech fans. They had gone wild in the terminal waiting for us, tearing down drapes and breaking out windows. The pilots diverted the plane to Amarillo and it was announced we were landing there. The crowd thinned out at the Lubbock airport and then we finally came back and landed.

"His talk about beating Texas was just like him," John Scovell said. "It was catching. He made us believe in ourselves and our game plan. He worked at the psychological level, which was where we had suffered. There was a barrier at Tech about Texas but he tore it down. There's not a player who played for Grant Teaff who was surprised by what happened at Baylor in '74. That was no miracle to any of us.

"I think he invented motivation. It's difficult to express in words how he could fire you up. He even had you enjoying grass drills on the hottest day. He had you feeling it was best for the school.

"You play over your head when you play for Grant Teaff, but you're well coached and well prepared. He has a super balance in everything he does, both in football and in his personal life. When he came to Tech he immediately identified with the players. Every guy, whether he was a starter or a redshirt, felt he could go to him with any problem."

John Conley, a Tech assistant coach who formerly coached in Grant's hometown of Snyder, took a special interest in him during his years on the Tech staff. No one better appreciated his feeling for the players.

"Grant's a fighter," Conley said. "He's personable, friendly and easy-going but you sure as heck don't run over him.

"One time one of our other coaches mistreated one of the players Grant had recruited. The other coach kicked him or cussed him or something. We were in staff meeting right after that, and Grant jumped the guy.

"Man, Grant was mad. Well, that coach told Grant if he didn't like it, just step outside. Before he got it good and said, Grant was on his feet heading for the door.

"Coach King jumped in and calmed them down. The guy was quite a bit bigger than Grant, but Grant didn't care. He didn't kick and cuss his players and he'd fight anybody who did."

I'll never forget that incident. One big reason I won't is that right after that I learned that son-of-a-buck had been heavyweight boxing champion of the entire U.S. Navy. But I felt very strongly about it and evidently he did, too. That coach and I have since become close friends. He became a successful high school coach and a couple of years ago I spoke at his football banquet.

John Scovell remembered Grant's great influence in the growth of a Fellowship of Christian Athletes chapter at Tech. "Until he came we really had no support from the coaching staff," he said, "but when he appeared it really came alive. His religion was in wonderful balance, too. He wasn't holier-than-thou and didn't wear it on his sleeve but you knew where he stood."

I've worked strongly with the FCA at all of my schools. The Tech chapter mushroomed the first couple of years I was there and by '68 it was one of the largest in the nation. I was especially pleased that summer when a group of the athletes accompanied me to an FCA Conference at Estes Park, Colorado. We shared an experience that has had a profound and lasting effect on my life. We heard a winner in athletics talk about winning in life. The speaker was Brian Sternberg.

I've always believed I am a winner. I believe you should act and think like a winner. You should plan and work and strive to the best of your ability in whatever you're doing and believe you're going to do it. I learned a valuable lesson about winning from Brian Sternberg. I learned that you can be a real winner if you put God in the center of your life.

I don't care how many championships you win or how successful you are in your endeavors or how much money you make, you're the biggest loser who ever came down the pike if God is not in the center of your life. No one I know ever proved this more emphatically than did Brian Sternberg, an astounding young athlete who for a few brief but brilliant months in 1963 was the greatest pole vaulter the world had ever seen.

I attended the national championship meets that summer with my top McMurry track athletes and I first met Brian when he was on the threshold of his greatest performance. I was on the field watching my long jumper, Bill Miller, warm up when Brian caught my eye. He was one of the finest looking athletes I had ever seen. He was a sophomore at the University of Washington, still a teen-ager, but he had a marvelous physique —6 feet, 3 inches, over 190 pounds, muscles rippling down his back. The poise and grace of his movements captured you immediately.

I saw him walk into the vaulting area, pick up a pole, take off down the runway, plant the pole and execute a flawless vault to qualify for the finals. Five other top athletes also qualified but you knew right then who would win.

The word around the track was that Brian Sternberg was the most self-centered young athlete to come along in a long time. He had won the national championship in the trampoline with a flawless triple somersault. In fact, he'd won everything he ever entered. The next day I was one of the first at the track because I wanted to watch Brian Sternberg perform. He didn't disappoint me. He not only won the pole vault, but he set a world record of 16 feet, 8 inches. The thing that caught my eye and my attention was his poise and confidence and the fact that he never smiled.

I kept thinking about that strange young man on my trip home to Abilene. He still was strong in my memory when I picked up the paper at the breakfast table one morning and was stunned by the headline: "Brian Sternberg Injured."

I hurriedly read the story and learned he had been working on the trampoline in the gymnasium at the University of Washington—by himself. He had attempted that famous triple somersault but he was a tiny fraction off. He came down on the edge of the trampoline on the back of his neck and almost completely severed his spinal cord. He fell to the floor, a helpless, hopeless cripple. He'd have died but a maintenance man found him, called the proper authorities at a nearby hospital and they rushed over. In the hospital the neurosurgeons and doctors examined and X-rayed him and said he couldn't live more than an hour. His respiratory system was faltering.

But Brian Sternberg was a fantastic competitor. He lived that hour. Then twelve hours, and twenty-four. The days stretched into weeks and then months. All the while he could move only his eyes and his mouth. His body, totally paralyzed, was in traction and was rotated every thirty minutes so his respiratory system could continue to function. He lay there, looking at the ceiling for thirty minutes and then at the floor for thirty minutes. He became embittered. You see, as human beings, when tragedy strikes if we don't move closer to God we move further away.

He was visited daily by a young girl. She had a different outlook. She had known Brian since elementary school and had never seen him smile. There was a boy with a vacuum in his life and all of his accomplishments could not make him happy.

She said, "Brian, what kind of relationship do you have with God?"

Brian really lashed out at her, and said, "I have NO relationship with God!"

Each day she asked him about putting God in the center of

his life now that all materialistic things were gone. Each day he refused.

Finally she left for several weeks on a family vacation. The first day back she came to the hospital and she sensed a difference as soon as she stepped in his room. She walked to the side of his bed, looked down in his face and saw a beautiful smile.

She thought he'd been told he was going to walk again but actually the doctors had told him he'd never walk. Why the smile? "I finally did what you suggested," Brian told her. "I put God in the center of my life and although I'm crippled I feel like a winner for the first time in my life."

It was a beautiful story and a beautiful testimony and Brian wanted to share it. When he could leave the hospital the FCA gave him the opportunity as their representative in the Northwest United States.

Nine hundred people attended that Estes Park conference where he would speak, a tremendous group of high school, college and pro athletes and coaches. But no one among them was more anxious than I to hear him. Just like when he vaulted for a world record five years before, I was the first one in the big meeting hall, waiting on the right-hand front row.

Finally everyone was seated and the hall was darkened. The light from a movie projector played on a large screen and there was that marvelous athletic image, 6-3 and muscles rippling down his back, picking up his pole, racing down the runway and executing that flawless vault.

Every coach and athlete oohed and aahed at that sight. Then the projector stopped. We sat in darkness a moment and then the curtains were drawn and a spotlight focused on a single empty chair with a microphone before it. I was wondering how they would get Brian out there when I saw a massive figure moving from the left toward center stage. It looked like a big football player carrying a little Charlie McCarthy wooden doll.

I was half right. It was a big football player named Wes Wilmer, who had dedicated himself to being the arms and legs of Brian Sternberg. And the Charlie McCarthy doll was Brian Sternberg. My young friend now weighed 87 pounds, his arms

As a small boy
in Snyder, Texas,
Grant looked on life
with keen interest.

Grant shows
football from Baylor
championship season
to Speedy Moffett,
his football coach at
Snyder High School.
(Paul Gilbert photo,
Snyder Daily News)

Back home for a visit during Grant Teaff Day,
the honoree relaxes with the people
who made it all possible,
parents Bill and Inez Teaff.
(Paul Gilbert photo,
Snyder Daily News)

Grant grew into star tackle and linebacker at McMurry College.

An extremely young head coach, Grant was just 26 when he took charge of McMurry football program in 1960.

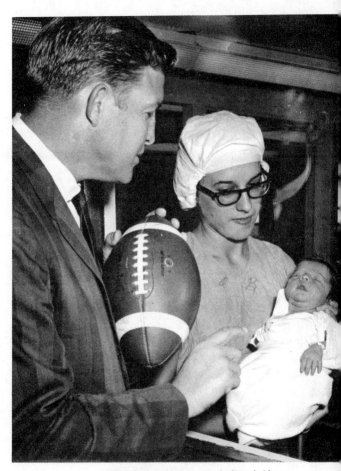

Proud father and winning coach, Grant holds game
ball after McMurry's opening victory as he admires
1-day-old daughter Layne on Sept. 12, 1965.
Players voted to give the ball to Layne.

e wreckage on runway at Shreveport,
fter Grant and his McMurry team
ved a terrifying experience in
mber 1963.

Moving into a new phase of his career, Grant became Texas Tech assistant coach in 1966 and helped the Red Raiders enjoy some rare moments.

Grant became Angelo State head coach in 1969 and quickly built a winning program. (*San Angelo Standard-Times* photo)

Grant spoke positively in his first press conference as Baylor head coach on Dec. 29, 1971 (*Waco Tribune-Herald* photo)

Western artist Jack White and
Grant admire White's painting of
Baylor Bear with a new image.
(Ray Cobb photo)

Grant knew
plenty of tense moments
in '72, but the final results
were surprisingly good.

Defensive coordinator
Pat Culpepper and
Grant reflect one of
many disappointing
experiences during
'73 season.

Grant was cheered by
Bob Hope's visit to Baylor
in '74 and pretty soon
everyone was feeling better.

Offensive coordinator Bill Yung, Grant and tackle Mike Hughes rejoice in final seconds of Baylor's comeback victory over Arkansas in '74. (Chris Hansen photo)

Baylor ticket manager Marie Abel, Grant and athletic director Jack Patterson shared the excitement of a sellout game in '74. (Chris Hansen photo)

Grant and Baylor players celebrate Texas' early scoring spree against A&M which assured the Bears of a spot in 1975 Cotton Bowl Classic. (Shelly Katz-Black Star, courtesy Time-Life, Inc.)

Grant shows historic headlines from Baylor's last championship season to players as they relax before watching crucial Texas–Texas A&M game on television on Nov. 29, 1974. (Shelly Katz-Black Star, courtesy Time-Life, Inc.)

Grant shakes hands with joyful Baylor fans after long-sought title and Cotton Bowl berth have been earned. (Shelly Katz-Black Star, courtesy Time-Life, Inc.)

Grant and the entire group hear those wonderful words from Cotton Bowl Classic official Field Scovell, the invitation to play Penn State on New Year's Day '75. (Shelly Katz-Black Star, courtesy Time-Life, Inc.)

Baylor's '74 starting backfield with their Coach of the Year. Above, from left: quarterback Neal Jeffrey, fullback Pat McNeil, Grant, tailback Steve Beaird, wingback Philip Kent. (*Dallas News* staff photo by Larry Provart) Baylor's championship coaching staff of '74 included, below, front row: Dal Shealy, Wade Turner and Bill Scoggins; back row: John O'Hara, Bill Hicks, Bill Yung, Grant, Corky Nelson, Cotton Davidson and Bill Lane.

Grant during anxious moment in Cotton Bowl game with Penn State, which ends Baylor's championship season on a strange note. (*Dallas News* staff photo by John Rhodes)

Joe Paterno came all the way from Penn State to visit with Grant and other famous Bears at gala banquet in Waco after American Football Coaches Association voted Grant national Coach of the Year in January '75.

Tracy Teaff brought a touch of women's lib to Baylor sideline in '74, serving as ballperson. (Shelly Katz-Black Star, courtesy Time-Life, Inc.)

Pinball coach at home above in family game room, Grant gives pointers to Layne, Donell and Tammy. Below, Donell and Grant watch youngest daughter Layne make her move. (Shelly Katz-Black Star photos, courtesy Time-Life, Inc.)

Family man Grant and his winning lineup:
Donell, Tracy, Layne and Tammy.
(Shelly Katz-Black Star,
courtesy Time-Life, Inc.)

dangled limply at his sides and his head swayed to and fro as Wes walked. Hanging over Wes' great arm were two skinny, bony legs. Once they were powerful pistons for this dynamic young athlete but now they merely were flesh, bone, cartilage and very little of that.

Wes walked carefully to center stage and gently placed Brian in the chair. He reached down, grabbed Brian's right trousers leg, pulled it over his left and dropped it. He told me later, "Coach Teaff, Wes does that to make me look normal."

They stuck pillows under his arms so he wouldn't fall out of the chair and slid the microphone close to his mouth so he could be heard. Brian's respiratory system was in terrible shape and he usually could speak only five or six minutes. Then he often would pass out. But he made the most of every second.

He told a beautiful story about a life filled with accomplishments and achievements and in the eyes of the world that of a total winner. But he had never felt like a winner until he put God in the center of his life.

His voice began to give way as he tired. His voice deepened and it seemed to me he leaned toward the microphone although I knew he couldn't. In a gasping voice, he said, "My friends, let me close with this: Oh, I pray to God that what has happened to me will never happen to one of you. I pray that you'll never know the humiliation, the shame of not being able to perform one human act. Oh, I pray to God you will never know the pain that I live with daily. It is my hope and my prayer that what has happened to me would never happen to one of you. Unless, my friends, that's what it takes for you to put God in the center of your life."

You talk about making the hair stand on the back of your head! What Brian Sternberg was saying to all of us, hale and hearty as we were, was simply this: One, he was glad that it happened to him; and two, if that's what it took for us to put God in the center of our lives, he hoped it happened to us. I'm certain no one who saw him and heard him that night ever will forget it. Everyone in our group from Texas Tech left with a clear understanding of what it really takes to be a winner.

8.

That Special Place

It was November, 1968, and Texas Tech had strong hope of playing in the Cotton Bowl on New Year's Day. Since an early 31–22 victory over Texas, the Red Raiders had increased their Southwest Conference record to 4–1 and were tied for first place. In his third football season as an assistant on J T King's coaching staff, Grant Teaff was excited about being involved in what could be the school's greatest year.

Then came the opportunity to move to Angelo State as head coach.

I had mixed emotions about the situation at San Angelo. I always had a special interest in the school because it was one of my alma maters. I played there when it was a junior college and I always appreciated the opportunity which Max Bumgardner gave me when no other school was interested in me. Max had continued coaching there through the years but since the school entered senior college football he had suffered with five losing seasons. Now Max was stepping out as a coach and Phil George, the Angelo State athletic director and another old friend, told me the job was mine if I wanted it.

The career goals which Donell and I had set years before

had called for a move to a head coaching job at a state college after three years as an assistant on a major college staff. From that standpoint the Angelo State offer seemed perfectly timed, but I found myself quite interested in staying at Tech.

The offer came right after we beat TCU, when we thought we had a chance to win the conference championship. Angelo State kept the job open and gave me time to think about it. Then the next Saturday Baylor destroyed Tech's dream.

That was John Bridgers' last team and he was under heavy fire, but he still had Baylor playing competitive football. Tech took a 42–28 licking and I took stock of my situation. The hope for a championship was gone and this clouded the outlook for the immediate future. I really had gone to Tech with the thought of some day succeeding J T King as head coach but I didn't know if staying there as an assistant now would help me or hurt me. I asked Jake and Polk Robison, the athletic director, what I should do.

Jake advised me the best way was to go out, do a great job and then come back to Tech. I still wasn't certain the San Angelo situation was right for me but in December I told Phil George I would like to be interviewed for the job. He set up an appointment with the school president, Dr. Lloyd Vincent.

Donell and I drove to San Angelo one afternoon, still doubtful about the venture, and our arrival in town didn't encourage us. As I entered an intersection a woman drove through a stop sign and our cars collided. We hadn't been there ten minutes and we'd had a wreck. After that, we just checked in at a motel and I called Dr. Vincent to delay our meeting until the next morning.

When I met him, however, I was encouraged. Dr. Vincent was very positive in every respect and I was convinced he would give his full support to help establish a winning football program. The school was growing and soon would become a university. Angelo State was committed to a building program and he wanted football to be part of it.

I still wasn't certain of my decision and I wanted to talk to an old friend. Brother Earl Sherman, who had been our pastor in Abilene, had moved to College Hills Baptist Church in San Angelo and I decided to drop in on him unannounced.

When I walked in he smiled and said, "Grant, it's good to see you. I've been expecting you."

I nearly fell through the floor. I hadn't told him I was coming to San Angelo for the interview.

We discussed the situation awhile and I told him of my indecision. Then he said, "I think you'll come." "Why?" I asked. "They need you," he told me.

I returned to the motel. Donell and I talked and prayed about it. Then we drove back to Lubbock and I told Jake I was taking the Angelo State job.

> Grant's impact on Texas Tech as coach, recruiter, scout and spiritual leader was noted when he left.
>
> "From strictly a technical standpoint, we can replace his coaching ability," King said. "But I don't think there's any way we can replace all those other things that Grant contributed."
>
> Wrote Burle Pettit in the *Lubbock Avalanche—Journal:*
>
> "A man of deep convictions, both religious and athletic, Teaff was a natural as a solicitor of talent, an image-enhancer for the entire college and, finally, as a teacher of the game.
>
> "And, trite though it may sound, Grant Teaff is a man whose word is uncontestable."
>
> Pettit concluded, "To replace Teaff in his strongest suit will not be possible. Such individual quality of character is, indeed, a rare commodity."
>
> A lot of people around Tech knew they were losing a good man.

Once we made our move we were delighted with it. San Angelo always was a great place to live and it still had the pleasant, friendly atmosphere I enjoyed as a student in the early '50s. But now it was a beautiful little city, and the school had changed tremendously.

The Angelo State campus was much larger than the one I knew in junior college. There was a new high-rise dormitory which the athletes moved into after I took over. There were more new buildings scheduled for the near future, including a football field house which I was allowed to design. The school was broadening its educational scope and was striving to do the same in athletics. It had just become a member of the Lone Star Conference, the top small college league in Texas, and everybody wanted to move ahead. But first we had to wipe out the negativism which lingered from five straight losing seasons and establish a positive program based on pride and confidence.

Obviously we had to upgrade Angelo State's recruiting program and I went to work on that pretty quickly, about ten minutes after finishing my introductory press conference. I made it clear, however, I wasn't trying to build a football factory.

"I'm interested in a program which is part of the institution," I said. "When a young man comes to our campus the first thing we want him to come for is an education."

That always has been my philosophy wherever I coached and it was part of the foundation on which I built at Baylor. Football can be a wonderful stimulus and rallying force for a school and its people but it's not the living end. It's just a part of the educational process.

We recruited well in those first months at Angelo State and it was fortunate we did. By the end of spring practice we were down to eighteen players and it helped to know we'd welcome some fresh material to our squad in the fall. We had established a strong conditioning program and our workouts were tough, as they had to be if we were going to improve. A lot of guys dropped out. The ones who finished the spring were with us all the way, though, and we set a goal of six victories for the '69 season. Around Angelo State that seemed an astounding number.

I soon formed an FCA chapter on the campus and it was well received. I try to let all of my football teams know and understand not through my words but by my actions that I am a Christian man and that they will have an opportunity to grow spiritually while they are members of the team. I am not pushy about it but they realize the opportunity is there. It's always interesting to see how they react to it.

At Angelo State there were some pretty rough customers on that first squad. One day one of them came to see me. "Coach," he said, "you have something I want." We talked and I learned that what he wanted was Christianity, which hardly is an exclusive possession. He was the first of five players who came to my office for the same reason.

By September our team had been strengthened by recruiting and we were eager for the season opener against Stephen F. Austin. After months of work, preparation and anticipation that team went out and saw SFA run up a 35–0 lead in the first quarter. Everything went wrong. I stood on the sideline thinking "What in the world am I doing at Angelo State?"

Despite everything, the players kept their poise. The second quarter was much better and the second half was great from the standpoint of execution and competitiveness. That early 35 points was too much to overcome, naturally, but our young men walked off the field with pride.

The next week produced my first victory at Angelo State but it was a loser in a way. We beat Sul Ross 20–19 on a late field goal but we were pretty beaten up. Three players were in casts and the course our season would take still was very unsettled.

That's how it stood when we faced my other alma mater, McMurry, in the season's third game. We played well most of the first half and led 6–0 with about two minutes left when we forced a punt. Then came a play which threatened to turn the game around.

Bobby Menchaca was one of the players who had stuck with us, a little senior defensive back who had known nothing but losing throughout his college career. Bobby was only about 5–6 and 145 pounds but he was eager to make something happen. In this case, too eager.

I sent him into the game to handle the McMurry punt and Bobby stepped back to our 10-yard line to wait for it. The ball was high and extremely long, however, and he started moving back for it. He was under instructions not to field a punt inside his 10 but in his excitement Bobby forgot where he was and grabbed it. Just then he was hit head-on by a big McMurry tackle. The ball shot out of his hands, into our end zone and McMurry recovered for a touchdown. They kicked the extra point and left the field at halftime with a 7–6 lead.

It was quiet in our locker room. I was anxious to see how Bobby would react. Well, he slumped on the end of a bench, dropped his head between his legs and started crying uncontrollably. I didn't say a word to him nor did anyone else. We started talking about the situation facing us in the second half but I kept one eye on Bobby.

About halfway through the halftime I saw his head come up. The tears still glistened on his cheeks but he was smiling from ear to ear. I was startled but I still didn't speak to him.

I was wondering about that smile when we left the locker room. Then Bobby grabbed one of my coaches by the arm and I heard him say, "I'm going to make it up to Coach Teaff. I'm going to take the next punt and run it back for a touchdown!" The coach thought he'd had a lick on the head.

Well, we kicked off, our defense held and McMurry punted again. It was another high one and Bobby stood on our 15-yard line waiting for it with McMurry players all around him. I yelled, "Fair catch it, Bobby!" But he didn't. He was determined to run with the ball.

I saw that 285-pound tackle right on top of him, ready to blast him as soon as he touched the ball and I turned my back. I didn't want to see what would happen next.

When I watched the game film I was amazed by what did happen. That tackle smashed into Bobby and knocked him back five yards but somehow Bobby kept control of the ball and his body. He twisted and turned and landed on his feet. He dropped down on his left hand, churned his feet and came up a little gap in the middle. He was hit again but he spun to his right. He was hit once more and he swung to his left. By now I had turned around on the sideline and saw what was happening and I was with ol' Bobby all the way. I yelled, "The wall, Bobby!

Get to the wall!" But Bobby wasn't interested in finding his blockers. He was only interested in reaching that goal line 85 yards away.

Twisting and turning, slashing and knifing, he kept escaping and moving upfield. Finally Bobby was alone and running free to the end zone. I've never seen a greater run in college football.

On the film we counted eight different times when Bobby was hit solidly. Eight times! He didn't have much speed but he had incredible determination and desire. It was a classic example of self-motivation. In those moments while he sat on the end of the bench, crying with his head between his legs, he realized he didn't want to feel sorry for himself and he didn't want our sympathy. I don't know what his hot button was but he found it and he pushed it. And that one wonderful play motivated the entire team. We beat McMurry and went on to the first winning season in Angelo State's senior college history.

Our record in '69 was 6–4, so we attained our goal. I was pleased by our progress. We were on our way now and all indications pointed to stronger teams each year. I felt I had strengthened my credentials as a candidate for a major college job but at the end of the '69 season I received a bitter disappointment.

There had been turbulence at Tech for some time. J T King retired from coaching and became athletic director. There at last was the job I had wanted but when we talked I realized I was not going to get it. There was too much pressure to hire a coach with a successful major college record and Jim Carlen of West Virginia was selected. It was a tough blow but I decided there was another plan for me.

Our life in San Angelo was grand. We were living and working with wonderful people, the atmosphere was invigorating, the achievements stimulating and the future bright. We had a lovely home and a lake house. We liked our church and our daughters' schools. Our blessings were many. But I knew that someday I wanted to be a head coach in the Southwest Conference.

In 1970, the first season Angelo State was eligible for the Lone Star Conference title, we had a solid, representative team.

Our record again was 6–4 but we showed marked improvement in both offense and defense. Our scoring increased 20 percent over '69 while we allowed one-third fewer points. Our recruiting continued to flourish and by '71—my third season—we were title contenders. The Lone Star Conference is perennially strong in football as you can judge from the large number of players who are drafted and play in the NFL. So our 7–3 record was significant improvement, particularly when you consider that this included a 38–21 upset over Texas A&I, the small college national champion. We had a good team, of course, but each player seemed emotionally right for that game.

In the pre-game devotional I offered a positive thought which everyone could use in his life: "I am only one, but I am one. I can't do everything, but I can do something. That which I can do, I ought to do. And that which I ought to do, by God's grace, I can do." That seemed especially appropriate for the occasion.

We had four all-conference players—offensive tackle Rodney Cason, fullback Jerry Austin, punter Bill DeMent and linebacker Thomas Williams. And our young tailback, Charlie Franklin, was LSC Freshman of the Year. Everything was on the upbeat at Angelo State and there were strong signs that '72 would be our first championship season. As encouraging as it was, however, I had to feel somewhat distracted once Jack Patterson contacted me about the opening at Baylor.

I had known Coach Patterson for more than twenty years. His hometown is Merkel, about seventy miles from Snyder, and after he graduated from Rice he coached successfully in Merkel as well as at San Angelo High School before he became assistant football coach and track coach at the University of Houston in the mid-'40s. He was a UH coach and I was a senior at Snyder High School in 1951 when we first met. He was on a recruiting swing through West Texas and dropped by our school. We visited but he didn't offer me a scholarship.

By the time I started coaching at McMurry he had moved to Baylor as track coach and I came to know him very well and developed a great respect for him. I was young and trying to learn and Coach Patterson always was most kind and gracious to me and helped me in my recruiting as well as my track coaching. He continued to do this after he moved to Texas in '63. He was always there, friendly and considerate and ready to help. What impressed me so much about Coach Patterson was that as long as I have known the man I've never heard anyone say one derogatory word about him.

When he returned to Baylor as athletic director early in '71, I was very pleased because of his reputation and his influence on people involved in athletics. I felt he would do an outstanding job. His move changed my attitude about Baylor. When I left Texas Tech the Baylor job was open and I can say that by no stretch of the imagination was I interested in it. Three years later it was open again and because Jack Patterson was there, I was interested.

Gray-haired and fatherly, Jack Patterson is a tall, lanky man of gracious manners and soft words. He earned a tremendous reputation as a track coach and in the process proved an unusual motivator himself.

Baylor always had been an also-ran in track until he moved there in 1956. Then the Bears promptly became contenders in a sport dominated by the University of Texas. He guided Baylor to its first championship in 1960, repeated the feat in '62 and '63, then accepted Darrell Royal's offer to move to Texas and rejuvenate the Longhorns. He also served as Royal's assistant athletic director but still won three more Southwest Conference track titles before returning to Baylor in January of '71. Through all those years he had developed many fond impressions of Grant Teaff.

"I was first aware of Grant as a high school football player," Patterson said. "I'd have to put him in a class with Roger Goree (Baylor's all-America defensive end in '72): He didn't go about anything half-heartedly. He was a competitor on the field, in the classroom, in club activities.

"I really came to know him when he was coaching

track at McMurry in addition to his many other duties. I thought he performed near-miracles because he had athletes who I'd classify as rejects or seconds, but he had outstanding teams and performers. He also had outstanding football teams. Although he had to operate with zero budget he still was competitive. I think many coaches in the Southwest Conference recognized his great talent but J T King was the first to approach Grant with something that would be attractive to him. Grant did a wonderful job for Texas Tech in so many ways, then took over at San Angelo and also performed near-miracles with a struggling program. So I had been aware of Grant for a long, long time.

"I'd heard him speak, been with him at coaching clinics and track meets. I'd had a chance to know him as a man and knew what he stood for. I knew there were so many pluses about him.

"Track is a unique sport in that you get to know the athletes on the other teams so well. You soon learn what they think of their coach. I knew from talking to guys at McMurry like Bill Miller and Freddie Fox that Grant not only was a great coach but a man who had their complete confidence. They felt he was fair and anything he said was law. When you put these things together over a period of years you can learn a great deal about a man."

Patterson filed his unusual knowledge of Grant Teaff for possible future reference when he returned to Baylor, a move which surprised some people.

"The first time I came to Baylor as track coach," Patterson recalled, "many of my friends thought I was crazy. But I recognized some things Baylor has to offer which are unique. It has so much more potential than a lot of people think it does. I felt good about leaving Texas to come back as athletic director.

"I wanted assurances on two points. One, that we would have a consistent budget. Two, that we would upgrade Baylor's athletic facilities over the next several years. In the past Baylor had had a yo-yo budget. In a good year you could get a lot of things and in a bad one you'd get zero. Actually, your greatest need for money comes during the hard times. If you can't get it then, you can't survive. And we had to have improved facilities if we hoped to be competitive in the Southwest Conference.

"I felt if we had assurances on those points then we could concentrate on getting all the Baylor people to join together and *stay* together one time. If we accomplished that we could do just about anything we set our minds to do."

Abner McCall, the Baylor president, told Patterson he would give him greater authority than anyone ever had before and that was all Jack needed to draw him back to Waco.

But there was an obvious question about Bill Beall's future as football coach, since after two years of a three-year contract, he had won only 2 of 21 games. And McCall didn't give Patterson the answer until late in the fall of '71.

McCall went into the hospital for removal of his gall bladder plus some minor surgery and he thought everything would be routine. Complications developed and he was hanging to life by a thread for weeks. But before he got in the critical state he decided there had to be a change of football coaches and named a committee to work with Patterson in selecting a new man.

"It had to be something of a crash program because this decision was made so late," Patterson said. "Some schools decide early that there will be a change at the end of the season if there is not improvement and in this position they have time to do some research on coaching prospects before they try to hire one. This was not the case with us.

"It seemed we went through an eternity hiring a

new coach but actually it was about three or four weeks. There were complicating factors and we couldn't move full speed ahead.

"Everyone at Baylor felt the program had deteriorated to the point that we must have a major boost and many top people felt this called for as big a name coach as we could find. In a situation like ours we didn't get a lot of positive response, but I was surprised by some of the coaches who were interested in talking."

Jerry Claiborne, formerly at Virginia Tech and then an assistant at Colorado; Johnny Majors, then at Iowa State; Eddie Crowder, then head coach at Colorado; and Ben Martin, the long-time coach at the Air Force Academy, all were prominent names which passed briefly through the Baylor picture. Plus many more.

"I tried to assemble as much information as possible on what we considered name coaches who might be available on short notice," Patterson said. "Fran Curci at Miami was on that list. He had a fine record but he was Roman Catholic. I personally felt we could have a Catholic assistant coach or a Catholic professor but I didn't believe Baylor's head coach could be Catholic. This is an unusual school in its close association with the Baptist churches and ministers and you had to recognize and respect it.

"At various times we felt we were close to getting together with a number of major coaches but they were a little afraid of some of the things about Baylor, such as our rules. Some of them might like to bend an elbow and thought that could hurt them. They didn't want to be hypocrites about it and they didn't feel they should try to come in and liberalize. Personally, I don't think that would be as big a thing as some people think it might be.

"Finally, after going through a long list, we realized we weren't going to get the big name. Then we shifted our search to a somewhat different area.

"Rudy Feldman at New Mexico had received a lot of support. Everything I knew about Rudy was good and today it still is. He expressed very strong interest in the job and agreed on tentative contract terms and budget items. He was announced as the new Baylor coach one afternoon, but overnight he had a change of heart. He called me the next morning and told me he wanted to stay at New Mexico.

"At last I was in a position to talk very seriously to Grant. He was the first coach I had contacted and I always had liked him. When this first started I had asked him to visit and he came to Waco. I gave him a tour of the facilities and tried to be as frank as I could about what we had and didn't have and our hopes for the future. He was very interested and so was I, but I had to speak frankly with him about his chances for the job.

"I told him, 'I'd like to hire you today but if I did they'd run us both off.' And I believe that was true at that time.

"But after all the problems we encountered, Feldman's rejection opened the door for Grant to join us. It was the greatest thing that ever happened for Grant and Grant was the greatest thing that ever happened to Baylor."

When Jack first invited me to visit the campus I understood he definitely wanted me but that he must work with a committee whose members had ideas about hiring a major college coach. I learned later from Dewey Presley, the chairman of the board, that Jack continually talked about me, keeping the committee conscious of my name if not excited about it.

He felt he would have a hard time selling a coach from a small college. The first time he called, he asked about my record at Angelo State. I told him we'd had a 7–3 season. He was pleased with that but said, "I'd give anything if you were coaching at some place like Morningside College in Iowa." He felt if I were from out of state it would have been easier to sell me with that kind of record.

Angelo State was not well known because it had not been a four-year school very long. People outside West Texas did not know what kind of record we had, even though we had knocked off Texas A&I, the small college national champion, and had three consecutive winning seasons. Coach Patterson understood the significance of our record but he was under tremendous pressure from the board to go after a big name. I think some of them may have thought he could have Knute Rockne reincarnated.

When I visited him in Waco early in his search he told me his thoughts about what Baylor needed for its future and I learned he already had in mind the things I thought the school needed to build a winning program. That was a five-year budget that he could live with as athletic director. He had talked to the administration and it was guaranteed.

He told me if I came to Baylor that he would go to bat to see that I had every tool to win with. That stuck in my mind and I kept feeling better about Baylor. I believed Jack Patterson knew what it took to have a winning program. He had been associated with Darrell Royal and the Texas program.

I felt good about the possibilities but I was not overly impressed with Baylor's facilities. In fact, we had built better facilities at Angelo State. But based on what Jack said, I felt that could be changed.

Jack continued to keep in touch with me. Frankly, I almost told him to forget it because I could tell he was having a tremendous problem with the committee. He kept saying, "You're the man I'd like to have and I'd like to work this around where I can offer you the job." I said, "Fine. I definitely would consider the job, for two or three reasons." I didn't tell him, but he was definitely one of the reasons.

Throughout this time Donell stuck with her real deep conviction that we were supposed to go to Baylor. She held firm although she had not seen the campus in years, didn't know anyone there and really hadn't heard much from me because

I didn't know much to tell her. I couldn't get enthused because there was a strong possibility I would not get the job. It was amazing to me that she persisted in saying that I would. Even the night we heard on the ten o'clock news that Rudy Feldman had taken the job she said, "I think you'll get the job."

"As Jack Patterson continued to stay in contact with Grant I looked more seriously at Baylor," Donell explained. "I realized he was very well suited for the job. There was no doubt in my mind he could handle the coaching part but there was a great deal more to it than that. Baylor had to have a man who could sell an athletic program, who could sell a dream, and who could sell possibilities for the future. Baylor had to have a man with some charisma, a man of confidence and a man with a very positive attitude and positive words for them.

"Being a Baptist deacon, layman and speaker had to be appealing in some ways and, of course, he also was a very fine football coach. I saw that, logically, Grant had to be the man for the job.

"We were getting excited about the possibility but then it was announced that Rudy Feldman had the job. I think Grant dismissed it from his mind then, but I felt so very strongly about his being suited for the job that I told him again I really felt we would be moving to Baylor.

"A very strange and eerie thing happened then, because the next morning I heard Rudy Feldman had rejected the job. I called Grant at the office and I never shall forget how stunned he really was when I told him the news."

It was about 3:00 P.M. on December 23 when Jack called me. I was in my office with an athlete I was trying to recruit. He asked me to charter a plane and fly to Waco that night because Baylor now would offer me the job.

He met Donell and me at the airport and drove us to his

home where we could talk comfortably. Things started on a bad note, however.

Jack, of course, was anxious and I guess a little nervous to get things worked out. I was excited about the possibility and wanted to hear what was to be said. When he pulled his car in the driveway, I got out on the right side. Donell was in the back seat so I opened her door and stepped back on the grass to let her out. We went in the house and visited in the den awhile. Then Jack suggested he and I move into the living room and talk business. We were sitting on a couch talking earnestly, but I kept smelling this horrible odor. My first thought was that a mouse had crawled under the couch and died. I could hardly listen to Jack for smelling it.

Then it occurred to me that he could smell the same thing and he might be wondering if I had a dead rat in my pocket. We exchanged glances and just then I crossed my legs. On my left heel I saw a huge piece of dog manure that I had stepped in on the grass. I looked down and saw that I had tracked it all the way through the den and living room. Jack and I laughed about it but I've never been so embarrassed in my life.

So we interrupted our discussion and cleaned up the manure and deodorized the house. We knew we had to hurry because Herb Reynolds, the provost and executive vice president, and two members of the faculty committee were coming by to meet me. Just as we finished spraying the house they rang the door-bell.

This was the first time I had talked to any of them. I was hired strictly by Jack Patterson. I hadn't been interviewed by the committee and never had talked to any member of the university administration. Everything happened strictly on Jack's recommendation. Without question, he is the person who brought me to Baylor University.

I was given a five-year contract and Jack wanted to announce my hiring that night for many reasons. It was important to make the proper newspaper deadlines and since it was almost Christmas some of the public might miss the news if we waited much longer. I was anxious to go ahead, too, although I would have liked an opportunity to sit down with my president back at

Angelo State. But I had alerted Dr. Vincent when I flew to Waco, so he was not terribly surprised by the news.

Dr. Vincent, of course, was disappointed that I was leaving but he is a tremendous person and a great leader. I think he sensed my desire to achieve at Baylor as I had at Angelo State and he was most gracious in arranging a release from my contract, which had two more years to run.

An announcement was prepared concerning the Baylor job and I talked to Dave Campbell, sports editor of the Waco paper. He quickly gave the story to the wire services and it was announced on the ten o'clock news that I was the new head coach. On Christmas Eve morning the story was in the papers and I'm sure there were plenty of puzzled expressions across Texas. A lot of people didn't even know I was being considered although there had been a few blurbs in the paper about me. Certainly the major papers in the state, particularly in Houston and Dallas, were not too familiar with Angelo State's program, or McMurry's either. Across the state the general reaction was, "How in the world do you pronounce that name? Grant Who? From Where?"

Of course, I knew this would be the reaction and it did not bother me at all. But I was concerned about our daughters' reaction to my taking the Baylor job. We called San Angelo to tell them the news. Their reactions were mixed.

Tammy didn't want to leave San Angelo. She was quite upset. She was a cheerleader in junior high school and had all the involvements of a typical teen-ager.

Tracy, who's always been adventuresome, said, "Let's go and teach them to be winners!"

And Layne, who is a tremendous competitor and the sorriest loser in the world, said, "Daddy, I want to ask one question. How many football games did Baylor win last season?"

"They won one game," I told her.

She was indignant. "I don't see how you could even consider going to a place that won only one game," she said.

"Honey," I told her, "that's one of the reasons we need to go."

9.
Starting the Climb

It was a chaotic Christmas for Grant Teaff and his family. After accepting the Baylor job he and Donell returned to San Angelo and found their home phone ringing constantly. It rang throughout Christmas Eve and until noon Christmas Day, when they took it off the hook while their family ate dinner. By then there had been 400 calls from people offering congratulations or seeking a job on Grant's new coaching staff.

That uninterrupted ninety minutes during Christmas dinner was the last calm time he would know for a long time. He was already busy organizing his staff and soon he would be off to Waco again for his first official press conference as Baylor coach. It was the start of a successful relationship with the media covering the Southwest Conference.

"Teaff handled himself like a champion," Dave Campbell wrote in the *Waco News-Tribune* after that first session of questions and answers. "What he did mainly was be himself.

"He has youth, good looks, a good smile, an earnest, sincere manner and a certain charm. It's easy to understand how he could be, as Tech's J T King has described him, 'a terrific recruiter.' He's articulate and in fielding questions he showed poise and an ability to think on his feet. All these qualities are sure to stand him in good stead."

Grant's outlook was positive, yet properly realistic and determined. This certainly helped his early impression in this demanding new job.

"Pronounce it Taf," said Galyn Wilkins of the *Fort Worth Star-Telegram*. "And don't laf."

Noted Roy Edwards in the *Dallas Morning News*, "Grant Teaff conveys the definite impression that there's no hill too steep for a stepper."

Everything wasn't positive, however. "This is super," said one cynic. "Now we can refer to Baylor as Grant's Tomb."

But Dr. Herb Reynolds, the university's provost and executive vice-president, made it clear at that first press conference that they were planning to build anything but a graveyard.

"We have reached the point at Baylor where we have to stand face to face with reality," Dr. Reynolds declared. "We have to provide consistent support for our athletic program in general and football in particular.

"We (the administration and trustees) have come to the conviction that if our program continues to decline in some areas in athletics, and especially in football, even our academic program will begin to falter.

"So we are going to support Jack Patterson and Coach Teaff and our other coaches in a definite and consistent way because we are convinced it is in Baylor's best interests to do so."

Grant treasured that commitment from his new school. Now he wanted to hire the type of coaches who could help him make Baylor glad it had made it.

In assembling my staff the first thing I considered, as always, was each coach's basic philosophy: his Christian philosophy, his attitude toward his family, his attitude toward people. Personality is so important. To coach for me, a man should not necessarily be some dynamic individual who comes on real strong, but one who is genuine and honest and wears well with people.

Then, of course, I also was looking for coaching skill. The question in everyone's mind was, could I assemble a staff that could compete in recruiting and on the football field? You could be the greatest Christian coach in America but if you're not sound technically and can't teach the techniques it takes to win games then you are in trouble as far as football.

And the kind of coaches I wanted had to have a special desire. They had to be able to suffer a lot, keep the program together and overcome the adversity I knew we'd probably have before we could move up and win.

A Baylor coaching job wasn't the most attractive situation in the world. I made it very clear to everyone it probably would take us five years of the hardest, most heartbreaking work any of us had been involved in and we took a chance of being out on our ears if we didn't do it.

I tried to mesh together a staff of nine coaches with varied experience and knowledge. I wanted some with major college backgrounds, some with small college backgrounds, some with high school backgrounds and, hopefully, one with a professional background. And in that group I also wanted some men who could give me a link to the Baylor history, Baylor traditions, and Baylor people.

I was quite pleased with the staff which emerged. It included three coaches from the high school ranks, because I always have been impressed with the quality of Texas high school coaches and felt if given a chance they could become outstanding college coaches. Contrary to what many people thought, I also felt they could become competent recruiters, largely because they were knowledgeable about which approaches appeal to young athletes. I decided they would recruit in the area of the state where they had coached because they would have the advantage of familiarity there.

But the first thing I did was invite two members of my Angelo State staff, Bill Lane and Wade Turner, to join me at Baylor. Bill was raring to go but Wade wasn't so sure.

Bill and I went back a long way together. We were the linebackers on San Angelo's junior college teams in '51 and '52 and years later he came back to join my staff at Angelo State after a fine coaching career at Daingerfield High School, where he won a state championship. He was on Christmas vacation in Denison, where his parents lived, when I called him and said, "I'm going to Baylor." "I'm going, too!" he told me. I told him he could become head coach at Angelo State and he was highly complimentary to me. "I don't want to follow you any place," he said. "I want to go with you."

I admired Bill as one of the best communicators with young people I've seen and also a tough disciplinarian. I told him he'd coach the defensive ends.

Wade had a different background and the decision to leave San Angelo was difficult for him. He was an assistant there before I took over and had suffered through some very hard times the previous few years. He had lost confidence in his ability. I sat down with him right after I moved there and we talked a long time about his getting off the ground and restoring his confidence. He had to realize he was not a loser because he had been associated with a losing program. He blossomed then and did a fine job, but he balked at moving to Baylor because he was set in his ways at San Angelo.

I gave him time to think everything out and then he accepted the job. As a result, Wade grew immensely as a coach and a person. He's very meticulous in his work and does a great job as defensive secondary coach.

Next, I interviewed coaches who had been on Bill Beall's Baylor staff. They were uptight and tense and I don't think I got a true picture of them. But after more investigation I knew I was interested in some of them and some others I wasn't. I learned from another coach I was interviewing that one of those coaches had told him there was no way Baylor ever would win the Southwest Conference title. I decided I would not consider that gentleman, because I feel very strongly you have to believe things yourself before you can ever teach them to young people. It was going to be a tough enough job for those of us who believed we could do it.

Some others looked like real assets to the staff and from that group I hired Bill Hicks to coach the interior defensive linemen, Mickey Sullivan to coach tight ends and Pat Culpepper as defensive coordinator.

Both Bill and Mickey were Baylor graduates as well as fine coaches and I felt their background could give our staff another needed dimension. Pat had a varied major college coaching background, having first been an assistant at Texas after playing linebacker for Darrell Royal in the early '60s. Then he moved to Tulane and Colorado before joining Baylor in 1969. He also was highly recommended by Jack Patterson, who said Pat had shown great energy and enthusiasm and had continued recruiting for Baylor during the long, trying period when the head coaching job was unsettled.

There had been no coordinators on Beall's staff but Pat sort of emerged as the leading defensive coach. He is a lot like I am in his intensity and energy. I like people who can work eighty hours a week and Pat can do that. When I told him I was going to keep him I made certain things very clear to him, as I did to all the coaches, about the conduct I expected at all times on the field and in all team relationships. I don't believe profanity has a place anywhere, much less on the football field. I try to let coaches coach, but there are certain guidelines I want them to follow.

Bill Yung, who became the offensive line coach, was a real believer. He was head coach at Grand Prairie High School and I spoke at his football banquet that December before I was hired by Baylor. He told me if I got the job he would like for me to consider him for the staff.

I didn't know him very well but began to check him out and everything I heard was great. And one thing which really impressed me at the banquet was a warmth from the players toward the coaches that you feel at very few banquets. This is the same feeling I believe you must generate to be successful.

Later Bill and I talked for ninety minutes and I was convinced he was exactly what I needed: inventive, ingenious, knowledgeable, and yet possessed with a rare depth and warmth. I'd coached the offensive line a lot because I think it's such an important part of football but I was so impressed by Bill I turned it over to him.

One of the first calls I received was from Cotton Davidson, who was a legend around Baylor. He had been a star quarterback there and also enjoyed a long professional career, first with the Baltimore Colts and later with the Dallas Texans and Oakland Raiders after spending one year on the Baylor staff in John Bridgers' first season, 1959. He also had coached at Oakland in the late '60s but left in order to live full time on his ranch near Gatesville. Cotton said he'd like to work for me but that he wanted to continue living on his ranch while coaching. I was flattered to hear from him but I was a little leery.

My first impulse was that he was semi-retired and wanting to run a ranch and also be a part of what we were doing. But I thought about it and decided it might not be too bad to have a guy so highly thought of and whose name meant something special to a lot of people. Cotton had a background as a professional passer and I knew I would have to develop my knowledge of the passing game because my teams had been pretty much run-oriented. Still, I thought he might be thinking of a job as a part-time coach, a weekend type, so I talked straight with him in our interview.

I told Cotton I would expect him to be a full-time member of my staff and expect him on time although he had a forty-minute drive to Baylor Stadium every morning. I held staff meetings early and we stayed late at night. He said that was fine with him. The more I talked with him the more impressed I became. Finally I offered him the job of working as receiver coach in spring training, leaving it to him to see if it was really what he wanted. I knew that after he went through a spring with me and through recruiting he'd know what kind of work was involved. Well, Cotton loves Baylor tremendously and wanted to join us. He worked out great and soon I had him handling our quarterbacks and the overall passing game. Our staff gained another valuable dimension.

I felt it was important for recruiting purposes that my staff include a top high school coach from the Texas Panhandle, so George Kirk of Amarillo Palo Duro was one of the first men I called. George told me he was more interested in staying in high school coaching and hoped to be hired at Temple, where he once coached early in his career. Later he called and said he wasn't going to get the Temple job and would like to come to Baylor. That was fine with me and I made him offensive co-ordinator.

I wanted eight coaches helping me with the varsity and a ninth to work with our freshman and junior varsity players. I offered the job to Bill Scoggins, who had just tied for a state title in Sonora High School, and he jumped at it. He had been in San Angelo and I knew of his work with young people. He was very close to his players, a good type for the job we had at Baylor.

So the staff was organized. We settled down for the long haul.

"Grant realized he was on a very hot spot," Jack Patterson said. "If he hadn't been a success early we would have been in a very bad situation.

"Before he took the job I had told him some cold facts. Baylor never had been able to unite all of its people and keep them united long enough to do the job. History told us that plenty of them jumped off the bandwagon at the first sign of hard times.

"I told him this job would test him sternly in many ways. There would be many people who, because of their deep interest in the school, would try to tell him how to run his business—recruit this player or that, hire this coach or that. I knew he had the ability to be tactful, to listen, and then do what he thought was right.

"I knew Grant had a unique ability to motivate young men and also to motivate adults. Any place

Grant appeared for the first time, on television or at a meeting, the Baylor people for the first time in years were proud to say, 'He's ours.' Grant is first class and this is what Baylor people like to see."

The only way I could hope to unify the Baylor people and change our public image was through personal diplomacy. I threw myself into it night and day.

In the first 120 days after taking the job I traveled 20,000 miles and faced 26,000 people eyeball to eyeball. I enjoyed a lot of it but the one thing I quickly grew tired of was repeatedly hearing people who really love Baylor telling those cruel jokes about the school and its reputation as a loser. And, if the people close to the school felt this way, you can imagine the attitude of the general public. The negative attitude horrified me.

There was a lot of lingering resentment over John Bridgers leaving Baylor three years before, although, typical of the division among Baylor people, there also was a camp which was all for it. But the handling of the Bridgers case had left a bad opinion with others. After he was fired and Bill Beall came in and did so miserably, I heard hundreds of high school coaches say, "Well, Baylor is getting exactly what it deserves." This was a big barrier to recruiting.

Now here I came, a fresh name with a different approach, and people seemed glad to see me and listen. Still, I was concerned about the negativism in their minds and knew this must be changed.

The media at every turn was wide open, receptive, and positive. One question I immediately heard concerned Coach Beall and his paint brush. He wanted to paint everything and give it a different look when he came to Baylor. He intended it as a positive campaign but it had a negative effect. At a news conference in Dallas in late '71 I was asked if I planned to paint everything at Baylor. I didn't know the full situation then but I gave an answer everyone seemed to like.

"Paint is only superficial," I said. "The root of our problem is much deeper. We must go to the heart of the matter—attitude, finances, facilities, the whole gamut." But I never said anything derogatory about Coach Beall and his program. I don't believe you build anything by tearing something else down.

The days, weeks, and months became a blur as I pursued this personal diplomacy while also working as hard as I could at recruiting and coaching. When I took the job I stressed that I must have great mobility and Baylor allowed me to lease an airplane, which was available with a pilot any time I needed it. This was invaluable because of the schedule I had to meet.

I might fly to Houston, speak at a Bear Club meeting and do some recruiting, then fly back to Waco that night. I'd get to the office about midnight, go through my mail, use a dictaphone to answer it and leave instructions for my secretary and coaches about work to be done in the office. Then I called my coaches wherever they were around the state to check on recruiting. They expected me to call them at 2:00 or 3:00 A.M. in their motel rooms. They'd bring me up to date and I'd decide where I needed to be the next day. Since I always hit it early the next morning, sometimes I just fell asleep at my desk. Don Oliver, our sports information director, likes to come to the office early. The first morning he came in at 6:30 A.M. and found me slumped over my desk it really scared him. He thought I was dead.

And during the first weeks I also tried to take off thirty minutes a day to look at houses. Donell and the girls still were in San Angelo, where she had handled all the details of selling our home, and I was trying to find a place we'd like in Waco. This was complicated by the fact that I didn't know which area we might prefer so I had to check out the schools as well. Every real estate agent within forty miles of Waco was calling the office, wanting me to look at houses, which could have been very time-consuming. Finally I found the right one on my own, a two-story, four-bedroom place perched on a hilltop overlooking a wooded area, a golf course, and Lake Waco. My family moved from San Angelo sometime in February and busy as I was I felt better knowing we had our home together again.

A negative attitude hung heavily over the Baylor players and I began attacking it as soon as I could. In our first squad meeting I made three points very clear:

First, I *wanted* to be at Baylor. I had a good job with a successful program at Angelo State but I left it because I welcomed this opportunity.

Second, I believed in Baylor and believed the athletic program could compete with other major universities.

Third, I wanted to build a program that would be an integral part of the university.

At the same meeting I outlined my basic philosophy, emphasizing that I believe in God, the worth of the individual, discipline, goals, and hard work. Thus we established communication quickly and I felt this was very important. For the immediate future these guys had to be the nucleus of our football team.

We were six weeks behind in recruiting when we started and overall it went very poorly for us. Only one blue-chip player visited our campus. Joe Washington, the great running back, was interested in studying dentistry and he seemed to like what he saw at Baylor. Of course, every school in the country wanted him and he wound up at Oklahoma.

This was before the NCAA imposed a limit of thirty scholarships per year on its members and in February, on the first day for signing letters of intent, Baylor at least came up with some impressive numbers: thirteen junior college transfers and thirty-six freshmen. Although we didn't kid ourselves about the strength of this crop, it still represented more quality than Baylor had signed in years. And we were confident we could do better in future years, when we would start even with other schools. We found our big disadvantages in recruiting were a lack of facilities and a losing image. Fortunately, both of those could be remedied.

That first group of freshmen, who would be our senior class for 1975, was generally weak but we still came up with some surprisingly good players. When we won the championship in '74 Pat McNeil was our starting fullback and Kenny Quesenberry was one of the best defensive backs in the league, being voted all-Southwest Conference and the Most Valuable Defensive Player in the Cotton Bowl game.

The fact that we brought in thirteen junior college players got a lot of attention. It seemed to start a trend in the Southwest Conference, where no school ever recruited a great many junior college players at one time. Baylor was a much improved team the fall of '72 and everyone talked about how much those players helped. Actually, only about five or six of those junior college transfers played much for us. Charlie Dancer best displayed what a transfer could contribute and he was the unlikeliest plus of all.

Charlie had played two years at Navarro and thought he was going to SMU but SMU decided they didn't want him. Everyone knew we were searching madly for players and someone called Wade Turner to ask if we'd consider giving Charlie a scholarship. Wade got some information on him and then called me. "He's not very big," Wade told me, "and he's not real fast and I don't think he can play defense. But he's a pretty nice kid." I said, "Bring him in to see me."

When Charlie walked in my office he really tested all my beliefs about not pre-judging a person. He was so skinny. Weighed 143 pounds and his little ol' arms were about three inches around. His hair ballooned with an Afro haircut. He gave me a big grin and there was a big gold tooth with a spade in the middle of it. As we talked I found myself really liking him.

He really impressed me when he said, "Coach Teaff, if you give me a chance I'll make you a great receiver. I'll do whatever it takes to win for you and Baylor. You won't be sorry you took me."

We were so thin I really didn't have much choice but to take him. It wasn't long before I was questioning my decision. Charlie had been involved in a very poor marriage and was in the throes of trying to get a divorce. He was broke, so he borrowed someone's car and an hour later we had a call from the police that he had rolled it out in a field and turned it upside down. In his first month at Baylor everything imaginable went wrong for him. But he was serious about making good his pledge to me.

Charlie was pretty slow for a wide receiver, only about 4.7 or 4.8 for the 40, but Cotton Davidson did a great job with him and he worked as hard as he could. He not only became Baylor's leading receiver but he also led the Southwest Conference. He became one of our great assets because he was determined to reach out for his potential, just as Neal Jeffrey was.

As unimpressive as Charlie was at first glance, Neal outdid him. In our early weeks we started an off-season weight training program and I'd come back to town from recruiting each Thursday or Friday and drop by, looking at the players and trying to get to know them better. I kept seeing this same skinny kid, sort of tall and dark-haired and about 160 pounds. I thought he was one of the managers. Every time I'd come close to him he'd duck his head and turn away. Finally I cornered him, stuck out my hand and said, "I'm Coach Teaff. What's your name?" He shook my hand real firm but nothing came out when he opened his mouth. I asked him, "Didn't you understand me? I'm Coach Teaff. What's your name?" I could tell he was trying to say something but nothing came out.

A coach who had been on the staff previously saw what was happening and nudged me. I walked to the side with him and he said, "That's Neal Jeffrey. He has a speech impediment. He was third-team quarterback for the freshmen last fall and not really that great an athlete but he has family ties at Baylor and wants to play here. (Neal's father, James Jeffrey, played halfback for Baylor in the late '40s.) I know he's real excited and upset about your coming up to him. Why don't you try to catch him later?"

I knew that eventually I would have the players visit with me individually to talk about their goals and I thought Neal might feel more comfortable then. He came to my office, sat down in front of me and it happened again. I would talk to him and he would stammer and stutter, the words seemingly caught in his throat. He kept trying, though, and after an hour and a half I finally got his goals out of him.

His number one goal was to be the starting quarterback the next fall when we opened the season. He was third-team quarterback on a sorry freshman team and he was sitting there stammering and stuttering that he wanted to be our starting quarterback as a sophomore. Talk about unrealistic goals!

But Neal wasn't finished. The last goal he got out really touched me. He said, "Coach, I'd like to be able to use my athletic talent so that I could some day stand and speak and tell what God has meant to me."

I thought about all of this a minute, then told him, "Neal, you know you must work to achieve those goals so get busy this spring." He nodded and left my office.

I've never seen anybody work like Neal. Cotton Davidson did a fantastic job teaching him quarterbacking techniques but you never saw a more willing pupil than Neal. When we opened the season against Georgia that skinny-legged, stuttering son-of-a-gun was our starting quarterback. He completed 18 of 30 passes against Georgia, the best game by a sophomore quarterback in Baylor history. It was the start of a brilliant career for Neal, both as a quarterback and as a person.

The next summer I was scheduled to speak at the Fellowship of Christian Athletes Conference in Estes Park, Colorado. I was waiting to be introduced when to my surprise gangly ol' Neal Jeffrey stood in an audience of 900, walked up on the stage and gave his testimony. I've never heard anything better in my life. Oh, he stuttered and stammered and those words hung up in his throat but everyone got his message. In essence he said, no matter how ugly we are, no matter how little talent we have, no matter how incapable we are, whether it be at speaking or singing or running or throwing, God can use every one of us. He loves us and he uses us.

The audience gave Neal a ten-minute standing ovation. He was tough to follow as a speaker, but it was a fantastic thrill for me.

My coaching staff didn't look at any film of the previous Baylor team. I wanted to make a fresh evaluation of every player in spring practice. As a result, we found several players who could help us. Tommy Turnipseede was one. He had come to

Baylor as a quarterback and spent the '71 season on the scout team. He wasn't even on the roster when I arrived, and he became an all-conference defensive back.

Such finds were the exception rather than the rule, however. I was terribly disappointed after our first few days of spring work. I had asked for and received a five-year contract because I thought that much time would be needed to build Baylor to a level that it could win a conference championship and play in the Cotton Bowl. After a week that spring I felt it might take ten years. I told my staff there were five players at Baylor who could have made Angelo State's starting lineup.

I've never been as disappointed in major college football players. Then, of course, I realized Baylor's recruiting had not gone well for the last few years. I knew that during my three years at Angelo State we never lost an athlete to Baylor. There were a lot of players at Baylor we wouldn't have considered at Angelo State.

In an evaluation by my staff at the end of spring practice we had thirty young men on full four-year scholarships who could not play winning major college football. And, just as we had experienced that first spring at San Angelo, there were some guys who didn't want to work as hard as we knew we must work to be competitive. They dropped out, so we moved them into another dorm and let them stay on scholarship. We didn't want anyone who wasn't positive.

Football is a contact sport and we had to develop hitting and mental toughness. I believe hitting and mental toughness are contagious, just as non-hitting and non-mental toughness can be contagious.

As the spring progressed, some players began to shed whatever was holding them back and come to the front. By the end of workouts we had found more who could be aggressive and competitive and play winning football.

Our goal was to find twenty-two hitters, and to encourage the players we instituted the star system. I carried green stars in my pocket and the first time I saw a lick I felt would be a winner in a game I stopped the workout, picked that young man up off the ground and stuck a star on his helmet. I don't know, that first one may have been just a case of a player tripping and falling into someone but he made solid contact and that was what I wanted to impress upon the players. It became contagious. All of the players wanted a star on their helmets. They wanted approval and they knew the way to get it was to be tough mentally and physically.

We played our final spring game on a Saturday night in April and drew a crowd of around 15,000, more than the attendance at most of Baylor's home games in '71. That was the last game in Baylor Stadium to be played on natural grass, or what was left of it. The stadium was like a dust bowl that night but we knew it would be different in the fall. The installation of AstroTurf began immediately after spring practice ended.

I told Jack Patterson when I took the job I was convinced we must make artificial turf a top-priority item in our campaign to upgrade facilities. He agreed and worked with amazing speed to raise the money to finance it.

I thought of the tremendous change in playing fields since I first reported for football at Snyder High School in 1947. It was late August and the first thing the squad did was pick the goatheads and cockleburrs from the grass. If we didn't get them out we knew we'd get them in our hands and knees when we were playing. It was a long way from cockleburrs to AstroTurf.

That was just part of a $400,000 program to give Baylor a first-class operation. Our athletic offices, which had been dingy and depressing, were completely remodeled and refurbished with paint, paneling, and carpeting. I felt that was essential because a young man's impression of a school can be set by his visit to the coach's office. Our athletic cafeteria was completely renovated and the stadium press box was painted and carpeted.

Green and gold aluminum chair-back seats were installed in certain sections of Baylor Stadium, which opened in 1950 and had very little maintenance since. Now its appearance changed rapidly and it became one of the most attractive stadiums in the Southwest Conference.

A lettermen's association lounge covering 5,000 square feet was built under the north corner of the stadium and it is one of the most beautiful you'll see anywhere. And the Bear Club's room, used by the alumni and booster organization headed by Catfish Smith, underwent the first of two remodelings as it continued to grow. Pride '72, the theme for our team, was taking hold everywhere.

So was Grant's campaign of personal diplomacy. During the final spring game the Baylor University Journalism department conducted a survey among people in the stands, asking them to fill out a questionnaire and turn it in as they left the stadium. Among the questions: How would you rate the image of Baylor's football program before Grant Teaff? How would you rate the image of Baylor's football program since Grant Teaff? How would you rate Grant Teaff in his public relations?

The answers: 92.7 percent rated the program's image before Teaff as unfavorable or extremely unfavorable; 87.6 percent rated the image since Teaff took over as favorable or extremely favorable; and 95.9 percent rated Teaff's public relations as favorable or extremely favorable.

"Our people were so starved and Grant made such a great impression touring the state," Patterson said. "That did more to stimulate our ticket sales than you could believe for a man who had yet to coach a game for Baylor."

Before the players left the campus for summer vacation we met and agreed on our goals. Our ultimate goals were to win more games than we lost, to play in a bowl game, and to bring recognition and honor to our school, student body and alumni by our actions on and off the field. Our intermediate goals were to play one game at a time, to do everything with pride, to maintain a positive attitude in words and actions, to develop team unity, to build confidence, to eliminate selfishness, to develop a Christian atmosphere, to improve leadership and

personal relations with others, and to better 1971's offensive
and defensive records.

Our immediate goal was an upper division finish in the
Southwest Conference standings and statistics, something
Baylor had not achieved in many years. Baylor had a great
tradition and I felt we should take from the past anything in
which we could take pride. We returned to the metallic gold
helmets, the kelly green jerseys, and white pants striped in
green and gold. I commissioned a famous Western artist, Jack
White, to paint a bear that would project a new image for
Baylor—an upright bear, head held high, a picture of controlled
ferociousness, rather than the snarling, blood-dripping-from-
the-mouth enigma. When the squad returned to open fall
workouts we wanted them filled with pride in everything they
saw.

From late December until July 1 I traveled over 50,000
miles, filled nearly 190 speaking engagements and talked to
approximately 60,000 people. I could see a great change in
attitude wherever I went. I was anxious for the season to
begin and see how much we could change on the field.

A Meet The Bears Night was scheduled for late August
shortly after we opened workouts and I was delighted to see
a huge crowd buy tickets to the barbecue so that they could
greet the team. I had been told that Waco people wouldn't
support football but I learned this wasn't so. An exciting
evening turned into a bad experience for me, though, when I
noticed Millard Neely was missing. He was a big kid, a
transfer of great promise who had been a junior college all-
American at Tyler. We had hoped he could move right in at
nose guard and give our defense a boost. I kept scanning the
crowd for him. Finally, just when everybody was eating
dinner, he arrived with another transfer, a running back named
Lester Ealey.

I was pretty unhappy that they were late and asked where
they had been. They told me they were leaving Baylor. We
had been going through three-a-day workouts and they weren't
accustomed to working that hard. Here were two players who

could help us and they were quitting. I told them to go back to my office and wait until I could talk to them there. Then, with that on my mind, I had to stand before that big crowd and introduce each player and tell something about each one. Somehow I got through it but I was in a cold sweat when I finished.

I went to my office and started talking to Neely and Ealey to learn if I could save them for our program. We talked about how hard we were working and I explained our goals to them and why this was necessary. I said they could help us but if they weren't right mentally I didn't want them. Neely was a giant but he was a sentimental type of kid. He started crying and said he'd stay and try. He did but he got hurt early in the season and didn't make the contribution we'd thought he'd make. Ealey stayed, too, and lettered that season.

The pluses far outnumbered the minuses, however. Baylor had won a total of three games over the past three seasons and we won five. We did it mainly by just hitting folks, playing a swarming defense, and being sound offensively. We lost six games but we were highly competitive against every opponent. Our leader was Roger Goree, a fiery redhead who became an all-America defensive end.

When I came to Baylor we knew Goree had been the best athlete on the squad for two years. We moved him from linebacker to end because we were going to run a five-man line and felt we had to have some strength to the strong side of the offensive formation. Our other linebackers couldn't play end but Roger could. By shifting he still helped us and the others stayed where they could help, too.

We developed a lot of confidence that season and it stemmed from an experience before our opener at the University of Georgia. This was the eighth-ranked team in the nation and we had to overcome a great deal before we ever kicked off. There were fraternity houses right behind our motel and they had rock bands playing at parties most of the night before the game. When we finally got to sleep, the switchboard operator woke us up to tell us an anonymous caller said a bomb had been placed in one of the rooms. The coaches got up, searched and found nothing. The players slept and they were ready to play the next afternoon.

It was 113 degrees on the field when we went out to warm up. Georgia timed its entrance so our players could see how awesome they were, a big splendid team in red jerseys. They're the Georgia Bulldogs and the stands were packed with about 60,000 of their fans screaming, "Dog meat! Dog meat!" We knew who they meant.

We were alone in the middle of all that but we had our pride, too. We cut our warm-up short because of the heat and I called the team together. I said, "Okay, we're going to walk right by those Georgia players and into our dressing room. When you pass them I want you to hold your heads high and your shoulders back and look at them. Get up high on your cleats so you'll be as tall as you can and walk right by them. I don't want any mouthing or talking. Just look at them and walk on by. They did and when it was time to come out for the kickoff I told them to walk again. It was hot and we needed to save energy. So they walked out and were ready to play. Georgia had a fine team and won 24–14 but we left that stadium with pride.

The next week at Missouri one of our captains asked me if they could walk on the field again. I told him they could crawl out if it would help. "Well, it made us feel good last week," he said. So they walked out and beat Missouri 27–0. We were off to a better year than hardly anyone dreamed we could have.

Baylor was a factor in the Southwest Conference race for a change. We lost a tough one at Arkansas 31–20 but then we beat A&M 15–13 and knocked off TCU 42–9, the first time Baylor had won in Fort Worth in eighteen years. So when Texas came to Waco the second Saturday in November we had a 2–1 record and actually could have tied for the conference lead by winning. We drew the largest crowd in Baylor Stadium history, 49,394, and went into the fourth quarter tied 3–3. Texas finally won 18–3 and went on to win the championship. Strange as it seems, we might have wound up 6–1 and gone to the Cotton Bowl that year if we somehow could have

gotten by Texas. The next two weeks we lost close ones to
Texas Tech 13-7 and SMU 12-7. Then we closed the season
by beating Rice 28-14. That gave us a 3-4 record and a fourth-
place tie in the conference race. We had led the nation in pass
defense, had the first sellout crowd in Baylor history, led the
nation in increased home attendance with a jump of 130 percent
and produced the school's first consensus all-America player
since '63 in Roger Goree.

But the most important achievement couldn't be found in
the headlines or statistics. That one was in our hearts.

In less than a year Baylor's new leader had gone
from Grant Who? to the Southwest Conference's
most celebrated football coach. The Texas Sports
Writers Association elected him Texas Senior College
Coach of the Year for '72. On the day it was announced Donell wrote this letter:

My dearest,

This is a very happy and very proud day in our
life and it's such a thrill for me to share it with you.
Logically I should jump up and down and beam
uncontrollably, for this truly seems a beginning for
what we hoped and planned in our life. However,
my joy is so controlled and channeled into complete
happiness that this new and great honor seems suddenly a very normal addition to an already over-
flowing cup! My cup truly runneth over with love
and excitement and anticipation in my life with you.

You've always allowed me to share every emotion
in your life—and in our profession there have been
many—and in our life together we've lived every
emotion that a full life can offer. There is so much
about you I love—your charisma so many feel, your
sensitive spirit and lovingness with our girls, your
energy, an adequacy for a "job to be done" that I've
never witnessed in any man, your gentleness, your
true and obvious love for each athlete, whether a

Goree or a redshirt, and, most of all, your God-centered life. I am very proud.

Thanks for sharing so much with me, and in these years just passed there have been so many proud moments. The only reason this day is different is that everyone in the whole world knows I'm proud today.

I love you!

D

10.

The Fall of '73

Most people remembered Baylor's surprising first season under Grant Teaff with a smile, then sat back and waited for more of the same in '73. The off-season was a delight. Recruiting improved remarkably. A fine crop of high school stars headed by Alcy Jackson signed with the Bears. Tall and fast, Jackson was a wide receiver sought by colleges throughout the country. Players like Tim Black, Flynn Bucy, Mike Ebow, Cleveland Franklin, Gary Gregory and Rell Tipton also added glow to the Green and Gold. Baylor fans, inspired by the turnaround under Teaff, set a school record when they bought 10,000 season tickets. That was 60 percent above the previous best sale, 6,300 in '63 when John Bridgers was the coach. All summer the Baylor people kept wishing the season would hurry up and start.

Then the season started and they wished it hadn't.

An opening 42–14 loss to Oklahoma before a sellout crowd in Baylor Stadium was a shattering experience. The Sooners exposed defensive weaknesses which would plague the Bears all season. There were critical injuries early and as the weeks passed Baylor's fate for that fall became grimly apparent. The offense was inconsistent, sensational at times and sadly lacking at others. By mid-season the team which had started the year pointing for a championship revised its goals downward, to trying to win a single Southwest Conference game.

Most of the TCU game was as discouraging as anything the Bears had suffered through all season. With a little more than 11 minutes left in the fourth quarter TCU led 34–7. But then the Baylor offense staged an incredible revival. The Bears scored three touchdowns and with two minutes left it was 34–28 and Baylor was driving again. When they made a first down on the TCU 15-yard line Grant Teaff began to think that something finally was turning out right.

This was our Homecoming game and I felt so strongly about what it means to the Baylor people that I had promised the crowd at Pigskin Review the night before that we would beat TCU. I reminded them that I had made only one other promise since coming to Baylor and I had made good on that when we beat A&M at Homecoming the year before.

As sorry as we had played against TCU most of the afternoon the team wouldn't give up. Then when those touchdowns came bang-bang-bang in the fourth quarter it was wonderful to see how it electrified the entire team and everyone in the stands. Now we had to get it across one more time to score one of the greatest comebacks in Southwest Conference history.

Neal Jeffrey, who had been performing beautifully, tossed a screen pass and our tailback, Gary Lacy, gained nine yards with it. Now it was second down and one yard to go from the TCU 6. I just knew we were going to win it. The next play lost four yards back to the 10 but I still felt good. We used our last timeout to stop the clock. With 43 seconds left it was third-and-5 and Neal came to the sideline to talk to me.

I told him to call 96 slant, a pass play we'd scored on many times. In fact, Charlie Dancer had just scored one of our three touchdowns on the same play. It was a great play in which both Charlie, our split end, and the wingback, Brian Kilgore, cut inside and flood a zone in the secondary. Neal would step back and drill the ball to one of them.

The noise in our stadium was tremendous as Neal and I stood together. All around us our players and coaches were yelling and waving their fists. We had been starving for a moment like this.

I wanted to be sure Neal realized we had to make the most of the remaining time if we didn't score on this play. "If they're covered," I told him, "throw it over that thing down there," meaning the scoreboard. "But," I added, "your tailback may be open." As an afterthought, as Neal ran back on the field, I yelled, "That's all of our timeouts!"

Neal went back to throw 96 slant but both receivers were covered. Instead of throwing the ball out of the end zone he dumped it to the tailback flaring out to the left. Gary Lacy had scored in this same situation a few minutes earlier when he grabbed the ball and cut inside. If he'd cut outside this time he'd have walked into the end zone but he cut inside again. He was hit for a 3-yard loss.

Now it was fourth-and-8 on the 13 and we had to hit a pass either for a first down or a score. But Neal somehow thought it was third down and he was thinking only of stopping the clock. I saw it coming, from the time he ran to the line of scrimmage and hurried the team to line up. I was horrified.

"Neal! Neal!" I screamed. He already was taking the snap from center, wheeling to his right and raising his arm. I wanted desperately to run out on the field and grab it. Then he threw the football. "It's fourth down!" I screamed, as if my words could bring the ball back.

The ball fell harmlessly near the stands. Our players looked dumbfounded and so did TCU's. Then the terrible reality of that moment struck Neal. He was in tears when he reached the sideline. "I thought it was third down," he sobbed. I tried to mutter something but I was in a state of shock. I couldn't believe we had lost our chance to win by throwing the ball out of bounds.

In our dressing room you could have cut the gloom with a

butcher knife. I stood in the middle of the room and looked at the players slumped on the benches around me. I saw Neal sitting there, his face down in his hands. He was crying so hard his shoulders shook. I realized that no matter how hard this loss was for us to accept it was nothing compared to the defeat Neal was feeling.

I hurt so bad I could hardly talk but I knew I must.

"I want all of you to know that I believe Neal did a fabulous job for us," I said. Neal still had his head down. I took a step toward him. I was trembling and tears were streaming down my face. "Neal! Neal! Get your head up!" I said. "Look at me!"

Slowly his head came up and his eyes met mine.

"Neal, I want to say I think you did a fantastic, unbelievable job. That's what I want to say."

In the background I heard players saying, "We love you, Neal!"

He looked at me and nodded. He was crushed. He felt the burden of the whole thing on his shoulders. It was so wrong because throughout the season he had been one of our greatest performers. I couldn't stand to see him broken by one nightmarish play.

It seemed so cruel that of all the quarterbacks in college football he should be the one to suffer this. He had worked so hard and overcome so much. It was tough enough that he constantly had to struggle with his stuttering and stammering, but it was worse that some people ridiculed him for it.

When we went to Fayetteville in '72 to open our conference schedule against Arkansas, one of the papers carried a story which said, "There was a field general who stuttered and he led his troops to the ocean. Before he could say 'Halt!' they marched into the ocean and drowned. Then there is Neal Jeffrey."

The morning of the game Neal and I talked about that story a long time. He was hurt deeply and so was I. He tried to shake if off but it probably affected his play that afternoon. We played Arkansas a tough game but we lost 31–20. A key factor was our failing to score a touchdown near the end of the first half after the Arkansas coaches figured out the hand signals I was using to call plays for Neal.

We used this system because we had found if we sent a player in with a message to call 42, Neal had trouble repeating it. When he received instructions from me visually he communicated more easily in the huddle. If I stood on the sideline and touched my right shoulder, that was 4. Then if I touched my nose, that was 2. Neal knew to call 42.

Trouble was that pretty soon Arkansas knew it, too. Frank Broyles' coaches in the press box figured it out and told him on the phone. In one instance, as we were about to run a play near their goal line, Frank ran almost to the end zone to alert his defense when I changed signals.

After that we decided to use signals only in emergencies. Neal worked very hard on vocal communication so we could send in plays. It was one of countless ordeals he had overcome to reach this point in his football career. But he always had a great attitude and he never complained. After that game at Arkansas the players were upset about the sportswriter who had written that story. One of them asked, "Neal, what are you going to do about it?" "I'm going to pray for him," Neal said.

After I heard that I told Donell, "That's the kind of quarterback we have. I wouldn't trade him for anyone else in the whole world."

When I dismissed the squad in the locker room after the TCU game Neal and I talked privately. I had had a lot of people questioning me about his ability to win, just the type of thing you get from people who know more about your business than you do. It hurt, because Neal's play had been one of our strong points. He was all-conference material. I didn't want him to lose everything he had gained because of that one crazy play.

I said, "Neal, I want to ask you a question. Do you believe you're a winner?"

Neal looked straight at me. "Coach," he said. "Do *you* believe I'm a winner?"

I told him I did, that I had complete confidence in him and that I believed he could win for Baylor. "That's all I needed to hear," Neal said. I meant every word I had told him. If I had any doubts at that moment, they involved me and not Neal.

Winning that TCU game could have been such a wonderful experience. Besides our great need for a victory and the fact that it was Baylor's Homecoming, the game and the entire week leading up to it had been filmed by the Southern Baptist Radio and Television Commission, which was putting together a series of documentaries on Christian men in athletics in the U.S. I was chosen to be the college coach. That really excited me because there are so many Christian coaches who could have been chosen. The director, a tremendous young man named John Stevens, had his crew shoot 90,000 feet of film that week. They covered me from all angles: practice, game, dressing room. They shot hours of conversation on my philosophy. I thought, "Man, what a fantastic recruiting tool this could be! We win this game and we have a great story to send across the country. Millions of people will see this." They followed me all the way but we didn't furnish the ending I had wanted.

As I left the deserted dressing room, the film crew was packing their equipment. I told John Stevens, "I'm sorry we didn't give you a winner."

I went to the press box for the interview session I hold after every home game. It was tough, not because of the questions the guys had to ask but because of how I felt. When we finished I took the elevator down and stepped into the darkness beneath the stadium. I heard something to my right and it startled me. I looked and saw Charlie Dancer. He had a tremendous game that day. He caught seven passes for 173 yards, a school record. He was leading the Southwest Conference in receiving and would become our only all-conference player that season but he wasn't thinking about that now. Charlie reached out with his bony little hand and grabbed mine. "Coach, I'm sorry," he said. "I'm sorry that we lost it."

Right then my heart touched his heart, because I knew how he felt and he knew how I felt. That helped, but I still had so much to overcome within myself.

I've never done as much soul-searching as I did after that game. I questioned my own ability and what I was doing at Baylor. I've never had a harder time recovering from a game than I did that loss to TCU. The hurt of that experience stayed with me well into 1974. There wasn't any reason we shouldn't have won it. To lose it like that was so painful. We had to play Texas at Austin the next Saturday and I probably did the lousiest job of preparation in my coaching career.

I would go to a workout or a staff meeting and I was listless. Negativism was building up within me. I preach against that and it was happening to me. I really had to fight with myself to keep going. I was upset because the defense hadn't played well all season. In seven games we had allowed 197 points. In eleven games in '72 we had allowed only 156. I wondered if I might even need to move Pat Culpepper out of the defensive coordinator's job right in the middle of the season. I was so filled with doubt and worry. I never had been through anything like that.

Besides all that, there were a couple of incidents which really hurt me. One outside the team and the other within.

I overheard two men talking about our program. I thought they were great friends and today I think without question they are, but what I heard that day tore me up. They were saying if I ever was to be successful I would have to do more coaching and less speaking. That really hurt and I thought maybe it was true, maybe I was spreading myself too thin. I try to involve myself as a Christian coach. I give of myself, day and night, trying to be used where I feel the Lord can use me. I didn't think this had been a mistake. Nothing had been said during the '72 season when we won so many games no one expected us to win. But when I heard that it created still another doubt.

We had a couple of players with bad attitudes who weren't contributing what they should in an effort to win and the other players knew it. They weren't of the strongest character and this disturbed all of the players who were giving us their best. It threatened to cause our entire program to deteriorate. One of those problem players was a heartbreaking case. He didn't have a daddy and for two years we worked with him in every way, trying to inspire him to reach out for his potential and to get an education. Well, he finished the season and then dropped out of school. Several weeks later he was arrested on a dope charge. It cut my heart when I learned about it. I had worked with him and my coaching staff had worked with him and we'd lost him. It was as deep a defeat as any we ever suffered on the football field.

With so many things building up and bugging me I went into the Texas game with a horrible mental attitude. It was the first time I had coached a game in Memorial Stadium at Austin and one of the big campus groups, the Cowboys, gave me a great welcome. They presented me with a pair of silver spurs and a big black hat. I looked on the hatband and saw they'd spelled my name Taft. I thought, "Yeah, they're real impressed with me."

Texas had another championship team and beat us 42–6, the latest in a series of dismal Saturdays which plagued us throughout the '73 season.

I had made a big mistake before the season. Some people had high expectations for Baylor because of that impressive performance in '72 and I let the enthusiasm build. I could see that unless everything went absolutely right for us that we'd face problems we didn't have the season before but I believe in positive thinking so I didn't say anything. And I got myself into a trap.

In '72 we had a lot of enthusiasm but we also had good techniques and real strong leadership from two or three seniors. Roger Goree, our all-America defensive end, was a dynamic leader and a playmaker. This was missing from the next spring practice. When we finished I knew we had two glaring weaknesses: defense and overall depth. Any injury to us would be critical.

But the Baylor people, bless their hearts, are the world's best about getting enthused. I had been cautioned about this. If you made two first downs they started yelling, "Green and Gold in the Cotton Bowl!" I should have tempered this enthusiasm but I didn't. I thought it would increase our season ticket sales, which it did. We quadrupled what we did in '72.

But I thought that maybe, just maybe, we'd get through the year without injuries and this enthusiasm would carry us through some tough times.

I believe in letting the players set goals, of course, but this carried them too high. The seniors had so many great things happen to them in '72 after seeing Baylor win only three games over the two previous seasons. They really got carried away. They set a goal of winning the conference championship and playing in the Cotton Bowl. I knew that was ridiculous.

By the time the Southwest Conference press tour came to Waco that fall I finally was beginning to express myself. I said, "We'll have a hard time duplicating last year's record." I don't know if anyone listened but I said it. The writers were enthused, too, and expected us to be improved.

We opened at home against Oklahoma and a lot of people put too much stock in the fact Oklahoma had just been put on probation and wouldn't be allowed to play in bowl games the next two seasons. They figured OU would just disintegrate and ol' Baylor would jump all over those guys and whip 'em. Actually, the only doubt about OU was the lack of a proven quarterback and that night against us Steve Davis served notice he was better than anyone they'd had before.

Our offense moved all right but our defense couldn't hold up. When we left the field our confidence had been damaged because of the mistake I had made months earlier.

We played pretty good the next week at Pittsburgh, where Johnny Majors was just getting his new program started, and won 20–14. That was only a temporary relief. Next we had to play at Colorado, which had enough talent to compete with Oklahoma. They wanted to beat us badly and they did, 52–28. Pat Culpepper once had coached there and they wanted to put it on him. And Eddie Crowder was fighting for his life as coach. I've never seen fans as rude and ugly to coaches as the ones that day at Boulder. They believed Colorado should have been winning some of those Big Eight titles Nebraska and Oklahoma had won.

Defensively we just couldn't hold anybody. That began to

discourage our offensive players. We came home to play Florida State, which lost every game that year, and we were very unimpressive in winning 21–14. By then the injury situation really had us down. In our first four games we lost seven starters. We couldn't stand up to that. We didn't have any depth. And we had very little leadership.

We opened the conference season in Baylor Stadium against Arkansas and our offensive statistics were staggering. Unfortunately so was our lack of scoring punch. We had 507 yards in total offense but scored only one touchdown. Dicky Morton got loose to score on runs of 68 and 81 yards and Arkansas won 13–7.

We should have been comfortably ahead at the half but we blew two or three scoring opportunities. I wanted so badly to win that game for a lot of reasons and it really got to me during halftime. The team had just left the dressing room to return to the field and I saw a Coke can on a bench. I was so mad I wheeled and kicked at that can. That proved why I never was a kicker. I was about three inches low. My foot hit the side of the bench, which was bolted into the concrete floor, and the impact jarred my whole body. Bill Yung was standing beside me and knew it almost killed me but I just walked out to the field. I wouldn't even limp. I made it through the second half but the next day I couldn't walk. The big toe on my right foot was broken and I had to wear a houseshoe. That was a real cute trick!

We had to play A&M at College Station next and I was trying everything to turn the team around. I played a recording of the Aggie War Hymn on the P.A. system all week, trying to get our players ready for all the noise and everything they would go through there. There was an incredible rainstorm during part of the game and fumbles hurt us badly, as they did so often in '73. A&M won 28–22, so when TCU beat us 34–28 the next Saturday we had lost three straight conference games by six points each.

Then Texas started another trend. We lost our last four by much larger margins.

We played Texas Tech before a wide regional TV audience

and the game had extra significance to me because it was in Lubbock before a lot of folks I knew real well. Tech clinched a Gator Bowl invitation by beating us 55–24. It was another weird statistical day for our offense: 29 first downs, 480 yards and eight fumbles. I also thought we were hurt by some unbelievable officiating. We had so many bad calls in '73, it seemed. I called the conference office so often I know they thought I'd lost my mind.

SMU was next and to show you what my mental attitude was by then I tried to make a deal with God to let us win. I pray a lot when I drive because I feel like I can really communicate with God then. So one day on the way to the stadium I said, "Okay, God, I want a sign from you. I'm working my guts out night and day to do this job because I believe you want it to be done. If you want me at Baylor next year I want to see a victory over SMU this Saturday!"

Man, I was trying to win! I wanted some help somewhere.

Later I told Donell, "If we don't win the next two games I don't believe I'll be at Baylor next year." She said, "Oh?" I said, "That's right. I told God if he wants me at Baylor I need to see some tangible evidence of his desire." She said, "I've heard you say a hundred times that football games are won on the line of scrimmage. God doesn't worry about football games. He worries about individuals who play football." Sheepishly, I said, "Oh, hush! I'm trying to win."

SMU won 38–22 but there was one bright spot. Steve Beaird rushed for 176 yards, a school record. We lost Pat McNeil, the regular fullback, with an injury before the Texas Tech game and I had moved Gary Lacy to fullback and Steve became the starter at tailback. Steve is a tremendous competitor and was real enthused about playing. He was a transfer from Blinn Junior College, this was his first year at Baylor and until then he had felt George Kirk, our offensive coordinator, was reluctant to play him. But Gary Lacy was a senior and George had a lot of faith in him, as I did.

The loss to SMU was our sixth in a row. By then I was mentally and physically exhausted but the season went from bad to worse. We went to Houston to finish the year against

Rice. I guess that was the only football game in my coaching career I've ever been ashamed of.

Rice had done pretty well in November and had some zip. They had a good defense and that day even our offense couldn't create a few sparks of life. They held us scoreless and won 27–0, the first shutout of my career. That really hurt but by then there was a long string of hurts.

It had been a miserable season. Baylor lost the last seven in a row, all in conference play, and finished with a 2–9 record. We finished in the conference cellar and last in defense, both in yardage and points allowed.

We were thoroughly embarrassed in that Rice game. In the dressing room afterward one of our top freshmen, Mike Ebow, said something that really impressed me. "I don't want to talk about what we're going to do next year," Mike said. "I just want us to do it."

I had told those freshmen when we recruited them and again on the opening day of fall practice that I believed they were the beginning of an historic era, that they were going to win a championship while they were at Baylor. Six freshmen started for us in '73. They were good, quality young men who never gave up. There was my big hope for the future.

But at the moment there were so many negative feelings pulling me down. We had to move right into recruiting and I was totally exhausted. I stood beside our bus outside the dressing room and my coaches came by and tried to express their feelings to me. I could hardly hold my head up. I told them I had nothing to say then but we'd get together as quickly as possible after we got back. This was the Saturday after Thanksgiving and I had told the players they could leave with their families after the game if they wished. Most of them did, so there were only three or four players with me and my family for the four-hour ride from Houston to Waco. My heart felt as empty as that bus.

I sat beside Donell and I was in total anguish. I began to cry. I felt so miserable.

"We've said all along that we really felt Baylor was where God wanted us to be," I told her. "But is this really the right place for us? Is coaching football worth what I've gone through night and day for two years, taking time away from my family and enduring all the physical and emotional strain? For this? Losing seven games in a row? Being humiliated?"

"I saw tears and I saw more pain in those four hours than I've seen in his whole life," Donell said. "But there was some relief, too, because the season finally was over.

"And I saw something beautiful happen before we got home that night. The tears were dried and he said, 'I know God brought me to Baylor. I've seen his hand in too many things the last two years. I know this is where he wants me. I know there is a job that I must do and perhaps the pain and the hurt and even the humiliation we have felt this season will help us as we begin again to build. We won't quit now.

" 'If I let down now,' Grant told me, 'I'll be letting down the team that came to Baylor because of me and because I had a dream of what could be done. And I believe that it can still be done.' "

We went home and spent most of the rest of the night talking. Together we asked God to give us the strength to do that job and the knowledge to know how to do it. We committed ourselves to whatever God had in store for us at Baylor.

By morning I had my head screwed on straight, my ears back, and my face in the wind. I was ready to get after it. I once told Neal Jeffrey, "Get your head up!" and he did. Now it was my turn.

11.
The Breakthrough

Jack Patterson recalled the relief he felt when he realized the Baylor people treasured Grant Teaff's overall ability enough not to lose heart after that dismal '73 season. "I didn't have one-tenth of the complaints I expected," he said.

"Some people I heard from were terribly upset, though. One guy called and said he was fed up and to cancel his name on the scholarship rolls. He said he'd been part of the frustration for twenty years and was getting out.

"I said, 'Look, if you alone quit we can live with that. But I know you well enough to know you'll talk this way to everybody you see. Your loss won't destroy us but the people you influence might.'

"The next day he called back. 'Pat, I want to apologize,' he said. 'I was a damn fool. You signed Grant for five years, so sign me for five. And I guarantee that everyone who has raised one word of protest will stick by you, too.'

"When everyone stayed with us after that 2–9 year I knew it would make a difference for a long time to come."

The season ticket sale for '74 was nearly 8,000, second highest in Baylor history and hardly a drastic drop from the 10,000 who purchased tickets with such high expectations for '73. And contributions to the athletic scholarship fund were a great example of the Teaff touch. In his first two years at Baylor the amount jumped from slightly more than $90,000 to $227,000.

The Bear coaching staff had another outstanding recruiting year, a strangely impressive situation for a school which didn't win a Southwest Conference game the season before. Defensive backs Ron Burns and Scooter Reed and offensive lineman Jon Kramer led a talented freshman class which seemed destined to help the varsity quickly. Baylor still was well received by high school coaches and athletes throughout Texas, indicating they were more impressed by Teaff's overall program than that poor second season.

After recruiting came an encouraging spring practice, featuring the arrival of new coaches Dal Shealy and Corky Nelson. Then came a summer which saw Teaff, after months of determined work for Baylor, revitalize himself personally.

"We were in Houston on a very hot day," said Donell, "when we passed a frail little black woman on a downtown street. She was leaning against a store window, asleep on her feet. She wore some old men's shoes much too large for her and her clothes were very tattered. On her head she wore an old rag. Probably everything she owned was in a grapefruit sack lying at her feet.

"Grant turned and looked back and tears filled his eyes. 'I wonder if she's eaten today?' he said. 'Do you think I would embarrass her if I asked her?' 'I'm sure you wouldn't,' I told him.

"He shook her shoulder and it startled her a little. Grant asked her if she had eaten. 'No,' she said, 'not for a couple of days.' He dropped some money in her hand and her eyes lighted up. I've never seen such joy in a person's face. She said, 'You're the first person in a long time who's stopped to care about me.' She was crying as we walked away. It really was a beautiful moment, because he did care.

"As we walked on down the street, Grant said, 'You know, our life is so good. We have so much and we should be so thankful. It makes losing some football games seem not nearly so important when you see someone who has the kind of problem she has. There's nobody in the world who wants or loves her.' "

While gaining a greater appreciation of his blessings, Grant profited differently from another trip.

"There was a calm and a peace that was very special during the season," Donell said. "I think it grew out of a week we spent during the summer on the campus of Oral Roberts University at Tulsa. We saw so many beautiful examples of what can happen if you trust the Lord day-by-day and don't worry about what's going to happen a week or two weeks or a month later. We got to know Oral Roberts quite well and could understand why he has inspired and helped so many people."

The school's founder, one of the nation's most renowned evangelists, headed the building of a strikingly modern campus which is permeated with positive thinking. Emblazoned in huge letters across the floor of the field house is his motto: "Expect A Miracle." Evidently Oral Roberts knew something *Texas Monthly* didn't.

A slick, well-written magazine published in Austin and dedicated to telling its readers what's wrong as well as right about the state, *Texas Monthly* devoted its September cover story to telling why Southwest Conference football was dying. The state schools in the league would continue to grow stronger while the church-related and private schools grew even

weaker, the article emphasized, noting that the
University of Texas' six straight trips to the Cotton
Bowl Classic illustrated the terrible imbalance which
already existed.

At the end of a refreshing summer Grant Teaff
read it and his eyes narrowed.

I've never been as irritated as I was by that story. It was so
contrary to anything positive. It didn't discuss how you can
solve problems. It simply said the problems were there and you
should just give up. The most absurd thing to me was the
thought that anybody should get out of the Southwest Conference. Anybody who wants to can be competitive in this
league.

That writer aimed his prongs at the church-related schools.
There I was putting my life's blood on the line to prove we
can be competitive and that private institutions have a place
and he was writing that we were dying and taking the conference with us.

It was so ironic that the year he proclaimed that Baylor
won its first football championship in fifty years. When we
were in Dallas in late December preparing for the Cotton
Bowl game, we were dining in the Venetian Room at the
Fairmont Hotel when that writer sent word to me that I'd
messed up his whole year. I wanted to see him personally but
he got out before I could catch him. I noticed when *Texas
Monthly* cited different people of distinction across the state
at the end of '74 they gave him the Bum Steer of the Year
award.

I can't say that I was certain we'd win the championship
when I read that story before the season, but I was confident
we'd be much more successful than we were in '73. The players
were more poised and experienced and they had set a reasonable
goal this time: to have a winning season and play in a bowl
game. Any bowl game. If they attained it, it would be Baylor's
first in eleven years but they were eager to try. So were the
coaches.

There were two changes in the staff after the '73 season,

both of them very important. George Kirk and Pat Culpepper, who had been the offensive and defensive coordinators during my first two years, left Baylor and I was faced with a major reorganization.

George had personal problems and felt extra pressure during the '73 season. He resigned in December and wanted to return to high school coaching. I helped him get the head coaching job at Plainview, Donell's hometown, and I was happy to see him do well there.

Dal Shealy immediately came to my mind as the coach I'd like to have fill that vacancy. He was head coach at Carson-Newman, a small Baptist college in Jefferson, Tennessee, and I had admired Dal for a number of years, both as a man and as a coach. Carson-Newman had played East Texas State for the NAIA national championship in '72 and Dal had a brilliant future in coaching. But he was very comfortable where he was, and there is a lot to be said for the tranquility of small college coaching. When I asked him to bring his wife for a visit to Baylor they had just built a beautiful home on a mountainside, the house they'd dreamed about for years. Dal knew he wanted to move into major college coaching some day but I didn't want him to come to Baylor and be unhappy. I tried to paint a bleak picture but it just isn't my nature to be pessimistic.

Dal is a very religious man with deep convictions. We had the same feelings about what could be done for Baylor on the football field. The longer we talked the more excited he became, but I wouldn't let him give me an answer. I told him to go home, settle down in familiar surroundings in that beautiful new home and make his decision. When he called and said they wanted to come to Baylor I was really elated because Dal was exactly the coach I wanted. He's a great teacher and technician and also he had the administrative background in college football to fill a new position on my staff as assistant head coach. That would take some pressure off me.

I promoted Bill Yung to offensive coordinator and Dal became offensive backfield coach, which meant he would work under Bill and yet be over him in another respect. But both of them are fine men and they understood I was seeking the best mixture of everyone's talents. It worked out great and our offense was far more effective in '74. We were more diversified, adding a split backfield and an option pass to our basic I formation attack, and Dal had a lot of knowledge in these areas.

In the spring of '74 Pat decided to leave and take the defensive coordinator's job at Memphis State. He was real upset about how our defense had trailed off in '73 after playing such a key role in our success in '72. He also felt badly about his poor results in recruiting. Pat was very intense and this sometimes worked against him. He had received a lot of attention in Gary Shaw's book, *Meat on the Hoof*, which was extremely critical of University of Texas football. In his book Gary Shaw criticized Pat for some of his actions when he was freshman coach at Texas, but it hurt Baylor's program because he was coaching there when the book was published.

Pat and I had talked about how our defense had lost something, whether it was in his relationship with the defensive team or what we were teaching. Something wasn't jibing and we had to play better defense. I told him he could stay at Baylor but to be perfectly honest he might not be defensive coordinator. He had spent five years at Baylor without a winning season and since his goal was to become a head coach it might be best for him to move to a new area and work with different people.

When Pat left I offered the defensive coordinator's job to Corky Nelson, the head coach at Tyler's John Tyler High School, the state AAAA champion in '73. Corky previously had been an assistant at North Texas State and was interested in returning to college football in a coordinator's job. He was able to join us for the last two weeks of spring training and it was apparent immediately he would be a valuable addition.

So we entered the '74 season with three coaches who were not on my staff when I started at Baylor two years earlier. John O'Hara, a fine young high school coach from Midland, had joined us as tight end coach in '73 when Mickey Sullivan had the opportunity to become Baylor's baseball coach. Mickey continued with our football program as recruiting coordinator.

Also, Skip Cox had moved from North Texas State to become our trainer after John Barnett resigned to enter business in Waco. He became a real asset to our program, an expert in training and conditioning athletes and also a valuable liaison man between the coaches and players.

By September we were working in a very encouraging atmosphere. There was a good chemistry on our staff and the players were confident. This was a team with renewed pride and one with more maturity and poise than any I had coached at Baylor. We didn't know we would make history but we did believe we could make up for some past disappointments.

The players were dedicated to having a good year. Tommy Turnipseede, who could have graduated, chose to come back and use his final season of eligibility because he wasn't satisfied with his performance in '73. He gave our defensive secondary a real boost. Dennis DeLoach, a regular defensive end until an injury made him miss all of '73, also was back. And Derrel Luce, who had suffered through a poor year at linebacker, became a great player for us.

I think we mishandled Derrel in '73. As a sophomore in '72 he had shown tremendous promise and it was obvious he would be our defensive leader after Roger Goree, our All-American end, graduated. But Pat Culpepper wanted to utilize the image of Goree and transfer it to Derrel by giving him jersey number 55, the one Roger had worn. I allowed him to do it and I even made the presentation to Derrel before the squad. This didn't inspire Derrel. He had worn number 46 and he wanted to be himself, not a re-creation of Roger Goree. He's highly intelligent and a self-motivator. He did not play well and he did not give us leadership. In the spring of '74 Derrel vowed he was going to become a great player. I gave him his old number 46 back and then Corky Nelson came in and did a splendid job of teaching Derrel some basic techniques we felt he could use. In the fall he was raring to get started.

Our build-up for the opener at Oklahoma was so good that you'd never have known by our players' attitude that they were tremendous underdogs. We surprised the country by playing well and trailing by only two points, 7–5, after three quarters.

Oklahoma finally won 28–11 but its starting offensive and defensive team played the entire game. Afterward, Barry Switzer came to our dressing room and congratulated us for the way we battled his team. It was a far cry from our opener in '73 when his guys threatened to run us out of Baylor Stadium.

Switzer told our players there was a very small difference between winning and losing and that if they continued with the same effort and attitude they'd shown that day they were going to be winners in '74. We left that dressing room with a lot of confidence, even if we did have an eight-game losing streak.

Baylor was playing at Missouri the next weekend and would leave on Friday morning. On Thursday Grant received the first copy of the 15-minute documentary film which had been shot the previous season. It concentrated on scenes during the terribly disappointing loss to TCU and in the emotionally-charged dressing room afterward when Grant showed such moving concern for Neal Jeffrey, the quarterback who killed a chance to win the game by mistakenly throwing the ball out of bounds on fourth down. When Grant left the dressing room that afternoon he told John Stevens, who directed the filming for the Southern Baptist Radio-TV Commission, "I'm sorry we didn't give you a winner."

"I couldn't tell him then," Stevens recalled later, "but they had given us a winner. I knew from what I had seen that this film would tell an inspiring and dramatic message."

I wanted to watch that film by myself the first time. When it ended, I cried for ten minutes. The film showed so vividly the anguish I felt after the game, all of the hurt for Neal. For almost a year I had fretted over that game and its impact on our '73 season. Now it suddenly was obvious to me how God can use a defeat as well as a victory. That defeat was worth all of the pain, anguish and humiliation everyone felt because of the countless lives it would touch with its great message. The Fellowship of Christian Athletes was going to distribute the film across the country and later it would be part of a series entitled "The Athletes" being prepared for network television. The message basically is that in life everyone loses some time or other and how you respond to that loss depends on what kind of person you are. It was so profound, so dynamic that I was very anxious to show it to the team.

I didn't tell anyone but I packed that film in my suitcase for the trip to Missouri. After we arrived on Friday morning I watched it again by myself. Then I called in the coaching staff and showed it to them. They all felt the same emotions I did.

But when I told them I wanted to show it to the players either that day or the next morning they cautioned me against it. They felt the team wasn't ready to see it yet and that it might hurt Neal's confidence. I had a gut feeling that showing them the film was the right thing to do but I succumbed. "Okay," I said, "I won't show it."

We played well against Missouri and I felt we should have won, but we didn't. Our offense was good in the first half and we controlled the ball but we gave up two touchdowns because our kicking game messed up and it was a 14–14 tie at halftime. Missouri began moving on our defense in the third quarter, scored one touchdown and was close to another one when Charlie McClanahan grabbed a fumble in mid-air and ran it back 96 yards to tie the score again. But our defense was sagging after being on the field so long and also running and whooping after Charlie's touchdown. Missouri drove for another touchdown in the fourth quarter and we lost, 28–21. That was nine in a row.

When we reached the airport and they were loading the plane I just couldn't hold back the tears. I wanted to win that one so badly and felt like we could have. I felt I had made a mistake in not showing that film. I sat on the steps of the little terminal building and cried. Donell and Don Oliver, our sports information director, were with me. Ol' Don really felt sorry for me. He'd never seen me like that.

But when we got home I felt much better. The game film

showed how well we had moved the ball. We just hadn't been fully prepared with our kicking game after moving some defensive players over to that unit. It was a mistake but we knew we could correct it. It was amazing how good we felt for a team with a nine-game losing streak.

Our home opener was coming up with Oklahoma State, which ranked eighth in the latest national polls, but I felt confident we'd play well. That Monday I was on my way to a speaking engagement when I thought of how fortunate I really was to have the life I did. I took out my notepad and wrote Donell this letter:

Sept. 23, 1974

Dear D

As I fly to San Antonio today my thoughts turn to you and I just wanted to express some things to you.

First of all, I love you more than I can ever show you. Especially during football season do you take it on the chin because of my dedication to what I am doing. I know how hard these last two years have been on you, but your love, attitude, and courage inspire me daily.

You alone keep me going and I thank you for that. Waking each morning and feeling your warmth near me and seeing your beautiful face turn me on for a new day.

I thank God for you and my beautiful girls every day of my life. Life is good, God is good and we are living the good life. God's got something good in store for us. We must work and wait. It will come.

Thank you for being you.

G

Late that night when I went home everyone was asleep. I placed the letter under Donell's pillow. Then I fell into a deep, comfortable sleep.

Oklahoma State was a big, strong team and undefeated, having knocked off Arkansas after it had upset Southern Cal. I felt good about our preparation all week, however, and I knew I would feel even better after I showed the players that film. After practice on Thursday I sent all of the coaches on the road recruiting, which is standard procedure before a home game. Then on Friday afternoon I called the team together and showed the film.

I said, "This film has a great message: that you can turn a loss into a victory. But that message will be meaningless if we don't come back and prove that Baylor can win, that Neal Jeffrey's a winner and that this football team is a winner."

The players were as touched by that film as I was. The next night they beat Oklahoma State 31–14. From the time they saw that film until the end of the season they won eight games and lost only one. Most of the time they played sound, solid football. Occasionally they played miraculously.

Oh, we had some tough scrapes along the way but now there was an air of confidence about this team, an ability to cope. Over the next few weeks a great new tradition was born as we frequently came back to win in the fourth quarter.

After we upset Oklahoma State that's how we won our next two games at Florida State and Arkansas.

Florida State hadn't won a game but gave a lot of indications of being dangerous. It was homecoming at Tallahassee and Burt Reynolds, who once played there, was back for the world premiere of his latest movie, "The Longest Yard." During the first half I thought that title must have meant our offense. Florida State led 17–0 and when we went into the locker room under the metal stands their fans were whooping and stomping and a rock 'n roll band was making a deafening noise right over our heads.

I told my coaches to stay outside while I talked to the players. I was upset but I was smarter than I used to be. I didn't kick any benches. I just slammed the door so hard it nearly came off the hinges. Everybody looked up and I proceeded to tell them very carefully how unhappy I was. To have a winning season we had to go back out and beat Florida State. They understood what I meant. Then the coaches came in and I called Dal Shealy and Bill Yung over. We decided to go more with our slot formation because Florida State had done a good job of defensing our split backfield. There would be lots of action for Steve Beaird at tailback and he was fired up. By now everyone was ready to go for the second half kickoff but when we reached the field the Florida State band was still out there giving its show.

That band must have stayed on the field 40 minutes and showed no signs of getting off. The director of the band was standing on a little platform and I walked up to him and yelled, "Get this bunch off the field so we can start the game!" Corky Nelson grabbed one of the game officials and said the same thing. I went to another official and started protesting but then I saw Leslie Benson, one of our really aggressive defensive linemen, grab the band director by the legs and start to carry him off. I went over and said, "Leslie, put him down!" Leslie is very responsive but sometimes he overreacts.

When we finally got on the field Philip Kent gave us a fine kickoff return out to the 40 and we were on our way to the first of three touchdowns which enabled us to win 21–17. We were glad to get that one behind us. I imagine that band director was, too.

A funny thing happened on the way to Razorback Stadium the next Saturday. We had spent the night in Rogers, a few miles from Fayetteville and so had Arkansas. A patrolman from the Arkansas Highway Department was escorting us to the stadium when he looked up the road and saw the Arkansas team being escorted by a deputy sheriff. Suddenly he took off and our bus driver stayed right behind him. We pulled beside the Arkansas bus, then went past and on to the stadium. Our players thought that was great. They jumped off the bus and started shaking that patrolman's hand. There we were in Arkansas' backyard and he led us to victory.

Then the game started and something happened that wasn't funny at all. Neal Jeffrey got cold-cocked. This left the quarterbacking to Mark Jackson but I had great confidence in him although he had been in for only a few plays all season. Mark was a sophomore of unusual ability, a transfer from UT El Paso who had spent a year at Baylor to establish his eligibility and also paid his way the first semester so that I could be certain he was serious about staying with us. When Mark first talked to me about transferring he said, "I want to come to Baylor because you're going to win." I knew the time would come when he would help us. He had a good arm and lots of poise.

Mark directed two touchdown drives and we led 14–0 before Arkansas scored to make it 14–7 at halftime. They scored 10 points in the third quarter and it was 17–14. Time began to be a real factor for us but strangely no one got upset. With two and a half minutes left we had no more timeouts and Arkansas had the ball on its own 40 but I looked at the players on our bench and I could see everybody believed we were going to win the game. Then there was a fumble and Wharton Foster recovered it on the Arkansas 36. Neal was ready to play again and moved us to a touchdown and we won 21–17. I'd never experienced a greater victory in my coaching career. And for a change Baylor was starting the Southwest Conference race with a win.

When you're hot you're hot and maybe it would have been good for us to play Texas A&M immediately rather than have an open date the week after the Arkansas game. The Aggies had become the favorite to win the title after beating Texas Tech, the team which upset Texas back in September. They were big and physical and had a tremendous defense. They easily had us out-muscled but we believed if we didn't make any big mistakes and played for the breaks we had a good chance to beat them. It was Homecoming at Baylor and we played before a stadium record crowd of 51,200 but fortunately I hadn't promised we'd win.

The Aggies scored two touchdowns, one when their fastest receiver, Carl Roaches, ran 56 yards after grabbing a fumble downfield which had gone through two Baylor players' hands. The other was scored by a defensive lineman, who intercepted a deflected screen pass late in the game and fell into the end zone. They kicked two field goals and won 20–0 although their offense never came within 15 yards of our goal line.

Afterward I felt we probably were too conservative against A&M and yet it was a good plan. They had been turning over the ball a lot in every game until they played us and then they didn't make any mistakes. We still had a good team with great morale, though, and our goal now was to be sure we went into the Texas game with only one conference loss on our record. The next week we went to Fort Worth and beat TCU 21–7 with a solid performance and we were assured of that position.

We had a 2–1 conference record and here came Texas, a school which had not lost to Baylor since 1956, the year before Darrell Royal moved there as head coach. The Longhorns were rolling now. Since that early loss to Texas Tech they had come back to play Oklahoma to a near standoff before losing 16–13 and they had grown stronger by the week in conference play. Two things had to happen the day we played Texas for Baylor to have much hope for a breakthrough. We'd have to beat Texas, of course, and A&M would have to lose, putting us in a tie for the lead. The Aggies were playing that same afternoon in Dallas against SMU, which was dangerous and capable. If ever there was a time for believing this was it.

We liked our chances but apparently nobody else did. A couple of days before the game the news leaked out that there had been a secret meeting of the Southwest Conference faculty representatives with some bowl officials. They were hoping to get a quick commitment from the Sugar Bowl to take either Texas or A&M, depending on which one didn't wind up in the Cotton Bowl. It hadn't worked out but the point still was made. No thought was given to Baylor although we still were very much in the race. Meanwhile, all the other bowls got worried about being caught short and filled up with teams that figured to finish with fairly good records. It was still the first week in November and the bowls were just about locked up and it was obvious Baylor was locked out unless we won the right to play in the Cotton Bowl.

I was really hot. Everyone just assumed we'd fold up and not be a factor. I told the players I believed SMU could beat the Aggies and then if they did the job I thought they could against Texas, people would start developing some respect for us. They went into the game feeling very determined and very positive.

I got so wrapped up in taking care of our own business that afternoon that I wasn't aware of the public address announcer telling our crowd during the second half that SMU had beaten A&M 18–14. By then we were staging the greatest comeback I've ever seen.

It was a gray, wet day but we believed we could throw short on Texas and then leave it to our receivers to try and break for big gains. Neal never passed more sharply. On the first series of downs he hit Alcy Jackson, who made a great run for a 69-yard touchdown. Bang! We were ahead 7–0.

But Texas came rolling back with awesome power. Earl Campbell and Roosevelt Leaks were running that Wishbone attack at us inside and Raymond Clayborn got loose outside when we had a defensive breakdown. At the half Texas led 24–7 and yet I've never been in a dressing room where there was a greater air of confidence.

I just told the players that they were giving a good effort, that I believed in them and that we still could go out and take charge. It was obvious what we had to do. We had to hold Texas scoreless while we scored a lot. We changed our defense, moving our linebackers up to where the Texas guards would have to try to block on them and drawing our corner backs up on the outside. Actually this gave us a nine-man front and we put Leslie Benson at middle guard to give us more beef and slow down their power. We had great confidence in our offense but we had to stop Texas from controlling the ball. We needed a big play early in the second half to give us momentum.

As we headed back for the field, I saw Neal and Dal Shealy praying together in the tunnel as they did at every game. I walked up and put my arms around them. Neal's prayer was the same as before: that he use his talents in such a manner on the field that he could be used by God in other areas. At another game the year before, the one with TCU, we had been far behind at the half and then come back only to wind up failing miserably. Neal had felt terrible after that game but he got his head up and never lost faith in himself. He believed he was a winner and so did the coaching staff. When he finished that prayer and went back on the field he had no doubts about his ability.

We got that quick boost we needed when Johnny Greene blocked a Texas punt and Johnny Slaughter recovered for us on the Texas 17. We soon had a touchdown and the score was cut to 24–14. From that point on we just kept the pressure on. Our guys played beautifully, the offense and defense constantly drawing inspiration from the other. We outscored Texas 27–0 in the second half, getting 13 points in the fourth quarter to win 34–24. That crowd in Baylor Stadium went bananas. Not only was this Baylor's first victory over Texas in 18 years but it opened a new door to us, one which could lead to the first Southwest Conference championship since 1924.

It was real wild on the sideline, too. It was an unforgettable experience, a far cry from that moment in the first half when I had blacked out. I was squatting when I saw Texas intercept a pass on a play which I thought was interference. I jumped up and sprinted out on the field about 10 yards before I realized a protest would do no good. As I turned back to the bench everything suddenly went black. My head fell and I crumpled on the AstroTurf. Some coaches and players rushed out to me but I was getting up by then. I simply had jumped up so fast that the blood didn't have time to reach my head. It was over as quickly as it happened and I was fine.

That was the only interception Neal threw that day. He gave his greatest performance as a Baylor quarterback, completing 20 of 31 passes for 351 yards and two touchdowns and running for another one. It was a classic effort in a classic game. So much had changed since that day he sat on a bench, crying his heart out after throwing away our last chance against TCU.

The end of the game was a beautiful experience. The entire stadium throbbed with happiness and emotion. Tracy, our four-teen-year-old daughter, had become a ball girl for the team that fall and she was on the field with me. We hugged and kissed and then I began looking for Donell. I knew she would be showing up in a second.

"Near the end of the game," Donnell said, "Tracy

had run up in the stands as fast as she could run and in full view of everybody screamed, 'Daddy wants to see you at midfield as soon as the game is over!'

"As I made my way down through the stands people were absolutely out of their minds. I met Grant at midfield and it was a very special moment because we shared a joy that I guess football coaches in particular know when a great victory is theirs.

"Even greater was that so many people had shared so much joy that afternoon. The Baylor people had waited so long to beat the University of Texas. I think that was their own special dream."

Afterward Darrell Royal did a tremendous thing. He came to our dressing room and congratulated us, telling the players it was great the way they never quit and that they deserved to win it. And he emphasized that they shouldn't look back. Now was the time to keep on winning. He's one of the truly great coaches in the nation and I have tremendous respect for him and his entire staff. He has a lot of class. For him to come to our dressing room after a game like that said a lot for college football.

And that evening, amid all the pandemonium at our house with people streaming in and the phone ringing constantly, a telegram arrived. It said, "Today everyone found out what we knew eight weeks ago." It was signed "The Oklahoma Football Team and Barry Switzer."

It's only human for any of us to enjoy tributes but as a football coach who had worked so long to reach where we now were these held a very special meaning.

It was the dawning of a new age for long-suffering Baylor people. The scoreboard lights stayed on until noon the next day and several of the university's trustees and administrators and their wives brought sleeping bags to the press box, where they spent the night gazing out at that marvelous message.

There were some strange scenes in Baptist churches

across Texas on Sunday morning. In Austin a man sat in the congregation proudly wearing the 1930 Baylor letter sweater he had dug from the mothballs. In Dallas the choir at the First Baptist Church filed in wearing green and gold robes. Then the director lifted a Baylor pennant in the air and led them in singing "That Good Ol' Baylor Line." Somewhere Billy Graham was smiling.

About 4:00 A.M. that morning Grant and Donell finally had gotten to bed. Donell felt an object between them and pulled back the covers. It was a Texas game ball.

12.
50 Years of Cheers

By Thanksgiving there was a Green and Gold glow to the Southwest Conference football picture. The drama of Baylor's success, climbing from last in '73 to first a year later, grabbed fans everywhere. And the fact that the Bears could bring the school its first championship since 1924 made them even greater sentimental favorites.

The lone opposition came from the Texas Aggies and their fans. With one game each left to play A&M and Baylor shared the league lead with 5–1 records but the Aggies faced an awesome assignment. They had to play arch-rival Texas in a nationally-televised game on the Friday after Thanksgiving and the site was Austin's Memorial Stadium, where A&M had won only once in fifty years. If the Aggies beat Texas they would qualify to play Penn State in the Cotton Bowl Classic on New Year's Day. If they lost that honor would go to Baylor whether it won or lost in its final game against Rice at Waco that Saturday.

Of course, Texas also felt keenly about its role. The Longhorns had a 4–2 conference record and 7–3 season record and wanted to finish strongly in the traditional game with A&M and move on to a post-season date in the Gator Bowl.

There was a story that Darrell Royal decided to pray about the situation. The Longhorn coach talked about the Aggies' toughness and finally said, "Lord, you are a Baptist, aren't you?"

"No," replied a voice, "but my beloved friend Grant Teaff is."

This brought some humor to an otherwise tense time for the Southwest Conference's three top teams. All of them realized, of course, it would be determined by who was most ready to play when the time came.

People talk to me about our playing eleven games in '74 and I have to correct them. I tell them we played twelve games and that one on Friday, before our Rice game, wore me out. All of the players and coaches gathered in the Letterman's Lounge at Baylor Stadium to watch the A&M-Texas game on TV and you could feel the emotion building as we sat there waiting for the kickoff. I don't believe our adrenalin would have been pumping any stronger had we been on the field taking pre-game warm-ups.

Thankfully, we didn't have to sweat out the entire afternoon wondering how Baylor would stand when it was over. Texas jumped all over the Aggies immediately, converted two fumble recoveries to touchdowns and led 14–0 before anyone could get settled in his seat. By the time fifty-four seconds were gone we knew Baylor was going to the Cotton Bowl.

Everyone was yelling, whistling and jumping in the Letterman's Lounge, naturally, but the entire town of Waco also went wild. Horns were honking, bells were ringing and people were running out in their front yards cheering and waving although it was a cold, rainy day. As soon as Texas got those 14 points on the scoreboard our ticket office was swamped with calls from people wanting to buy Cotton Bowl tickets. The excitement was incredible but pretty soon I tried to calm the players down. I was concerned that Rice would come in and destroy everything.

We continued watching the game, which Texas eventually won 32–3, and enjoyed every second but I was thinking about how I might best impress the players with the importance of being ready to play the next day. That night we checked into the same motel where we stay before each home game and I followed my usual custom of showing the team a film and then going from room to room and talking to the players individually. I stressed that we didn't want to back into anything. Since A&M and Texas both had two losses we could still lose to Rice and go to the Cotton Bowl because Baylor was the only school involved which never had been there and thus received preference. But we didn't want it that way. We wanted to be undisputed champions. We had worked so hard and achieved so much to this point that it would have been ridiculous to go out and allow the meaning of all this to be changed by a mediocre performance against Rice.

When I went to bed I felt we would be ready, just as we had been against Texas Tech and SMU.

There had been some questions about our ability to sustain our momentum after that wonderful victory over Texas. Tech and SMU were dangerous and a letdown could have ruined everything but we proved the poise and talent we had shown against Texas were not temporary.

We beat Tech in Waco 17–10 and we had to do it the hard way. They came out with a new offensive formation, using an eight-man line which flanked our defensive ends. By the time we adjusted to it they had driven for a touchdown and led 7–0. That was still the score at the half but our players had been asserting themselves. The play everyone remembered was made in the second quarter by Ron Burns, who had become a star defensive back in his freshman season. It was fourth-and-3 in our territory and Tech was trying for the first down but Ron stopped Tech's quarterback, Don Roberts, with a bone-jarring tackle which changed the mood of the game. The Tech offense never was the same after that.

We won that one in the fourth quarter, too, after Neal Jeffrey was injured and Mark Jackson took over at quarterback. Mark showed his poise under pressure again, marching us down the field for the touchdown to break a 10–10 tie.

That gave us a 6–3 season record with two games left so Baylor was assured of its first winning season in eleven years. The next afternoon I met with the players and we set a new goal: to win at least a co-championship. That we could do on our own, by beating SMU and Rice. We still had our other original goal of playing in a bowl game but we needed some help from Texas on that since the Cotton Bowl was the only one left open to us. Some others which might have been logical possibilities had hurried out and made commitments elsewhere. The Sun Bowl really upset me, expressing a lot of interest in Baylor for awhile and then easing off and indicating Oklahoma State might be invited. I didn't think that was right because we had beaten Oklahoma State by 17 points. The Sun Bowl people told me if Oklahoma State decided not to come, we'd be next in line. Well, Oklahoma State backed out and the Sun Bowl people never even called me. They invited Mississippi State and North Carolina. But now that was behind us and we were determined to deal as best we could with our actual situation.

With that in mind we went to Dallas and played the best overall game during my first three years at Baylor. The fact that we played SMU in the Cotton Bowl may have given us added inspiration. We sure played like a team that wanted to come back there on New Year's Day. I said during the game that we looked like champions and we did. SMU was a tough, talented team but we were mentally and physically prepared. We won 31–14 and the SMU people said afterward that not even Ohio State had controlled a game against them like Baylor did.

It was simply a day when so much seemed to go right for us. The crowd made it sound like a Baylor home game. So many people made the trip that someone painted a sign and put it on the northern outskirts: "Last One Leaving Waco Turn Off Lights." And we had a bunch of super performances from individuals. Aubrey Schulz, our center, did a tremendous job of blocking Louie Kelcher, SMU's gigantic nose guard, and Steve Beaird had another great day running through those holes. Neal Jeffrey hadn't worked out all week because of his injury in the Tech game but he completed the first seven passes he threw and gained enough that afternoon to set a Baylor career record for passing yardage. And Don Bockhorn, one of our regular linebackers, kicked a 59-yard field goal. It was another school record and came at a critical point in the third quarter when we needed to regain momentum.

Bockhorn, Schulz, Beaird and Philip Kent, who made a lot of big plays at wingback, were seniors in their second year at Baylor. All of them were junior college transfers and they played a great role in our improvement.

So as we left Dallas in November we knew it would be decided at Austin the next Friday whether we'd be coming back in December. Then Texas assured us we would and it came down to whether we could finish our season like true champions.

We had a tremendous air of confidence about us when we went on the field to warm up. It was a bright, clear day but had turned off real cold. The temperature was close to freezing and a strong wind had dropped the chill factor to 20 degrees. This didn't diminish our enthusiasm, however, nor that of our fans. The crowd numbered a little over 40,000 and about 8,000 of those had bought tickets in the last few hours before the game. This was to be an historic day at Baylor and they wanted to be part of it.

We beat Rice 24-3 and although our performance wasn't superb it was solid enough. If we hadn't missed a couple of good scoring opportunities in the first quarter the game could have turned into a rout. It was funny how everything had changed in a year. Baylor had ended the '73 season in humiliation at Houston when Rice beat us 27-0 and I cried all the way home on the bus, asking myself if I were in the wrong job. Now the band was playing "That Good Ol' Baylor Line" and thousands of our fans were standing and holding their right hands up like bear claws and singing. It made me tingle, and not because a cold wind was whipping in my face.

It was a great feeling to know we were Southwest Conference champions. We had brought something to people who wanted it and deserved it for so many years. We walked off the field and into the tunnel and found the entire ramp leading to our dressing room was covered with cotton bolls. It felt marvelous. And it was such a long way from walking off that field at Rice a year before.

During my post-game interview I was asked how I felt about my new five-year contract. I had to say I felt surprised, because I didn't know I had received one. It was announced in the press box during the fourth quarter but nobody had talked to me about it. And nobody in an official capacity talked to me about it after the game either. It was simply announced and then left hanging during all the celebrating and excitement about going to the Cotton Bowl.

I didn't give it much thought. I was busy rejoicing for a day which meant so much to so many and it was wonderfully appropriate that the date was November 30, Donell's birthday.

She and the girls waited for me while I held a special press conference in the Letterman's Lounge. When it was finished I walked over to her. "Honey," I said, "I forgot to get you a present but I'll do something for you later. How would you like to go to the Cotton Bowl game?"

The spin-off from Baylor's victory was fantastic. The school's fans set an all-time Cotton Bowl record by purchasing 36,500 tickets for the game with Penn State. The button and bumper sticker craze which began during the fall with "I Believe," the Grant Teaff motto, became an industry in itself during December. One of the new favorites: "I Believed But Now I *Know!*"

There was happiness everywhere and constant reminders of the Bears' success. On December 2 the annual Christmas tree went up in front of the Baylor Student Union Building. It was twenty-four feet tall and composed of 16,000 cotton bolls. Someone around Waco sure knew how to get those things together.

At a football banquet sponsored by the Baylor

Chamber of Commerce, longtime Longhorn loyalists Wally Scott and Don Weedon came from Austin to present a ten-foot-tall mounted Kodiak bear, wielding two vicious-looking claws. As it was unveiled, the crowd began to applaud as they saw the claws were covered by orange mittens.

So much was going right for Baylor. The '74 season was the first time the Bears had beaten Arkansas, Texas, and Texas Tech in the same year. There were individual honors at every turn.

Eight players made all-SWC teams: quarterback Neal Jeffrey, tailback Steve Beaird, wingback Philip Kent, center Aubrey Schulz, linebacker Derrel Luce and defensive backs Tommy Turnipseede, Kenny Quesenberry, and Ronald Burns. Jeffrey received the Kern Tips Memorial Award as the outstanding senior in the Southwest Conference and the Fort Worth Kiwanis Club Sportsmanship Award. Beaird, Baylor's first 1,000-yard rusher, was voted Texas' Amateur Athlete of the Year and the *Houston Post's* Outstanding Offensive Player. Schulz was named first team all-America by the Football Writers of America and second team by the Associated Press. Luce made second team all-America in the NEA selections.

And for his job of leading Baylor from 2–9 to 8–3, the greatest improvement of any major college team in the country, Grant received almost every conceivable honor during that dizzying December. He was Southwest Conference Coach of the Year, Texas Senior College Coach of the Year, UPI's National Coach of the Year, and the FWAA's National Coach of the Year. But he refused one honor that for years he dreamed of having: the head coaching job at Texas Tech.

When I went to Dallas to attend the Southwest Conference winter meetings the second week in December it became clear that Jim Carlen was leaving Tech for South Carolina. There was immediate speculation that Tech would offer me the job and I was quite concerned about the position this put me in, as well as all the people I love and respect at both Baylor and Tech. J T King, Tech's athletic director, is one of my really good friends in the coaching profession, the man who gave me my first opportunity as an assistant coach in major college football. I had told him that if I was going to be contacted about the job I wanted it done in total secrecy. I didn't want to be in a position of telling Texas Tech no or hurting my program at Baylor or being put in a position of bargaining with anybody. But everything kept building up and there was more and more speculation that I was a hot prospect for the Tech job. This was only logical, I guess, considering my background and past association with Tech.

After the Kern Tips Award Dinner on Friday night Jake asked me if we could talk before I went back to Waco. I told him at the outset that I wanted anything he might say to me put in almost nebulous terms. I did not want an offer. So we just had a general discussion about the job and the situation at Tech.

When I returned to Waco that weekend I realized the story was getting hotter and hotter around the state. The fact that I had yet to sign the new five-year contract Baylor announced for me two weeks before led to the assumption that I wanted to keep myself open to the Tech opportunity. Actually, I hadn't signed it because I had yet to see the contract. Nevertheless, by Monday morning the thing was running rampant. We were resuming workouts for the Cotton Bowl game that day and everybody was sitting around worrying about my moving to Tech.

I told my coaching staff I was going to make a decision shortly whether or not I wanted to be considered for the Tech job. Then two or three players came by to ask if there was anything they ought to know. I told them not to worry, that if there was anything they should know I would tell them. That afternoon we held our workout and I didn't say anything.

I went back to the office and told Don Oliver to call a press conference for ten o'clock the next morning so that I could clarify my position. Then I talked some more with some staff members and with Jack Patterson. Jack was very nice and also quite fair, talking about how good the situation was at Baylor but also encouraging me to get away from anyone interested in either school and then make my decision independently.

I went home to discuss it with Donell and the girls. Like any decision we've ever made the opinions were varied.

Donell, as always, was totally open. She said, "If you feel that's what you should do, then go. I'll be with you 100 percent."

Tracy wanted to go immediately. She's just adventurous. Tammy, who was a senior in high school and planning to enter Baylor the next fall, didn't want to go. And Layne was just aghast at the idea. She said, "Daddy, the only way I would go is if they change their name to Texas Tech Bears." I said, "Well, I don't think they're going to do that."

We talked some more and then I told them what I had decided. About 1:00 A.M. I called Jake in Lubbock and woke him up. I told him I was going to have a press conference the next morning and wanted him to know what I was going to say and exactly what my feelings were. I told him I wanted to have my name withdrawn from consideration for the job.

The next morning Jack and I were to have breakfast with Baylor's president and executive vice president, Abner McCall and Herb Reynolds. I went to our offices first and walked in wearing a black suit with red trim—Texas Tech colors. Jack saw that and almost croaked. But I quickly told Don and him my decision and he smiled. Don was so elated he cried a little bit.

Before we sat down to breakfast I told Dr. McCall and Dr. Reynolds that I was staying at Baylor. This was before I ever saw the new contract. After we ate and visited awhile they showed me the contract and we discussed a few things. I felt quite strongly about my coaches' situation. The salary scale at Baylor now is among the highest in the country. They asked me what we needed in the way of improving the program. I mentioned dormitory improvements and a new weight room. There wasn't any bargaining. We just had a good discussion and agreed on the direction we should go at Baylor. I feel if I do the job then the financial aspect will take care of itself. And

I feel if I've committed my life to a project or a school then I'm going to do a good enough job that the people in charge are going to believe in me and give me the tools to work with.

After our breakfast Jack and I returned to our office for the press conference and it was announced I had signed a new five-year contract, running through 1979.

So many people were concerned whether I would leave or stay at Baylor. As I was making my decision what stood out in my mind was the outstanding group of athletes we had recruited in the spring of '73. The only reason they came to Baylor was because I sold them on my dream—that it could be done and that Baylor would win a championship. I felt a deep commitment to them, and a commitment to Baylor. I feel if people believe in you and if they're committed to you, then I believe in turn that you are committed to them.

A lot of people think I made a mistake when I didn't move to Texas Tech. I don't think so at all. I'll always be confident I made the right decision. Baylor has a tremendous number of plus factors. The fact that we could win has carried over in our recruiting and there is the challenge of proving what happened in '74 was no fluke. My goal is to be competitive and have a good, strong program at Baylor, year in and year out. And I want us to be proud of who we are and what we're doing.

Jack Patterson could best reflect the great transition which both Baylor and Grant Teaff experienced in his first three years there.

"It would have been an utter disaster if he had moved to Texas Tech," the athletic director said, "for several reasons.

"Damage to the scholarship program was one. If we had a brilliant young man with great potential and lost him, a great many people would have thrown up their hands and said, 'What's the use? We had him and we let him get away. Why should I give my money and my time?'

"If he had gone and we had hired the greatest coach on the field in the U.S. he would have been held up consistently for comparison to Grant. People would have said, 'He can't speak. He can't recruit.' It would have been unfair to the new coach because Grant had captured the hearts and minds of every Baylor alumnus and every Baptist in the country.

"It would have been not only a blow to Baylor but a blow to all the private schools across the nation. People would have said, 'Well, a private school gets good men and it can't keep them.'

"Yet I can see how Grant would have been interested. Texas Tech is a fine school but Baylor University gives him a platform to do and say the things that might not be readily accepted at other schools. At Baylor he can speak in terms of his strong religious beliefs and how he thinks they are important. At other schools this might be frowned on or actually discouraged.

"So I think Baylor offers him many opportunities to do the things he believes are important, yet I believe all those things he does are important to Baylor. They might not be at other schools."

The appreciation which Baylor people felt for Teaff staying at their school was typified by a letter from alumni Martha and Harrel Spears of Lubbock.

"We just wanted to express our rejoicing that there are still men like you who feel dedication and commitment, loyalty and affection for an ideal. Naturally we are moved because we also love it.

"No alumni love their school more than Baylor people, and we certainly feel that your years there have made you one of us. Thank you for bringing victory, honor, and pride to her, reflected in measure to us in the 'jubilee year.' "

13.
Enjoying the Heights

The rejoicing went on and on for the Baylor people. There were some celebrations in most unusual places. For John Stevens, who had become a great fan of the Baylor Bears and Grant Teaff since directing the filming of their deeply emotional experience at the TCU game in 1973, his came in the sky over Japan. He was on assignment for the Southern Baptist Radio-TV Commission and knew that Baylor was in good shape after Texas beat Texas A&M but he didn't know the outcome of the final game with Rice.

"I was on Japan Air Lines flying from Fukuoka to Hiroshima the day after the game," Stevens said, "and the stewardess gave me the one English language newspaper on board. I found the U.S. college football scores at the bottom of the page and read every one until I found it: Baylor 24, Rice 3.

"I whooped and threw that paper to the ceiling. The Japanese are very quiet people and this startled everyone on board. They turned and stared. They probably thought, 'That American must be crazy.'"

There were also some celebrations at most unusual hours.

In the pre-dawn darkness of December 1, the morning after Baylor won the '74 Southwest Conference championship, Grant was jolted awake by a ringing telephone. He groped for it awhile and when he finally got the receiver to his ear, he heard a man yelling, "WE WON! WE WON! WE WON!"

"Yes, sir, *I know* we won," Grant replied, but do *you know* it is 3:30 in the morning?"

Sleepy as he was, he still had to appreciate that fan's excitement. When a school wins its first championship in fifty years you can't expect folks just to applaud a minute and then sit down. In Baylor's case the celebration endured through December and was going strong in the final days before the Bears met Penn State in the Cotton Bowl Classic. The Teaff family led the advance guard into Dallas, checking in December 26 and they brought with them warm memories of a Christmas much different from that chaotic one three years earlier when Grant had just accepted the job of trying to rebuild Baylor's football program from the bottom up. And Donell proudly displayed a special gift from her husband: a 20-dollar gold piece minted in 1924.

It was almost a shame we had to play that game. Getting there was so much fun and being in Dallas for the entire week of festivities was such a thrill for everybody that the game was almost anti-climactic. But the game really was very important, a valuable new experience which helped us to grow. And without it I wouldn't have had the opportunity to get to know Joe Paterno.

Joe is a prince of a guy and, of course, a great coach. When he brought Penn State to Dallas to play us he had the best career record in major college football. In nine years his teams had won almost 85 percent of their games, and they had lost only one bowl game in six previous trips. Joe isn't a very big man. He's about 5–10, has dark wavy hair and wears thick horn-rimmed glasses. He has been described as looking more like a librarian than a football coach but don't let his appearance fool you. Joe Paterno knows football and he knows people. He's a winner.

We were scheduled to hold a joint press conference a few days before the game and Joe had told some sportswriters that he was looking forward to meeting me. I smiled when I read that. We had met once before—very briefly.

It was at the Texas Sports Hall of Fame luncheon which is held every year on New Year's Eve. This was in '71, when Penn State was to play Texas, and just a few days after Baylor hired me. I went up to Joe and introduced myself. We shook hands and that was all there was to it. So really there was no reason why he should remember me at all.

My special feelings about Joe went back to that time. I wouldn't say I was awed then at watching Joe and Darrell Royal in Dallas that week but, of course, I was impressed.

I had always been impressed with Darrell and if I hadn't been impressed with Joe right off I certainly was after his team beat our conference champions 30–6.

> The two coaches were asked to discuss their individual approaches to player discipline because it was obvious there was a great contrast between them. At Baylor, the players lived closely together in the same dorm and observed a strict curfew, in bed and lights out by 11:00 P.M. and up for breakfast at 7:00 A.M. At Penn State, where there was no curfew, the players might live anywhere they wished. Tom Shuman, the star quarterback, chose an A-frame mountain cabin far from the campus. Paterno didn't see the difference as any big deal.
>
> "Oh, you do what you do," he said. "Obviously, Grant is more of a discipline coach than I am. I always want to do things when I want to do them and I figure the kids do, too.
>
> "Yet, I think your kids can smell a phony. A lot of

coaches couldn't get away with what Grant does, but it's real obvious to me that his kids believe in him and what he does."

We went to Dallas with every intention of enjoying the honor of representing the Southwest Conference in the Cotton Bowl and to participate fully in the week's activities. That's exactly what we did. Naturally, since Baylor is a Baptist-supported University, we made our own special plans for attending church the Sunday before the game. At the invitation of Dr. W. A. Criswell, I spoke at the First Baptist Church. Meanwhile, the team attended services at Park Cities Baptist. The day before we had attended a Fellowship of Christian Athletes breakfast which drew an overflow crowd of 1,000 to Texas Stadium Restaurant and since some people were suggesting Baylor hoped to pray its way past Penn State I used that opportunity to make clear my feelings about that.

I told the crowd, "I firmly believe that God will answer your prayer, although he may not always answer it exactly the way you want him to."

Then I told about a friend of mine, a wealthy young man who wanted just one thing in this world: a grizzly bear for the trophy room of his mansion.

Finally he found one place in the country where he could get one. He flew there and then went after that bear by himself. The bear was at the top of a mountain—the ideal place for a bear to be, incidentally—and this young man went up a narrow trail in search of him. Finally he saw this great beast and raised his rifle. He slipped on a rock, though, and almost fell off the mountain. Miraculously, he grabbed the edge of the trail and scrambled back up as his gun fell out of sight.

As he got up that bear was coming right at him. He started running but the bear was with him step by step, hot breath on the back of his neck. Finally he lost his footing and started tumbling down the side of the mountain. The bear was right behind him. He rolled head over heels for some time and finally came to rest on his knees.

Well, this young man besides being rich, articulate, and astute also was a fine Christian. He felt in this position, on his knees with the bear right on top of him, this was the appropriate time for prayer.

He bowed his head and prayed as fervently as he'd ever prayed in his life. "Oh, God," he said, "just make this a Christian bear."

When he opened his eyes he could still feel the bear's presence right on him. He turned and looked to his right and there beside him was this hulk of an animal, but on his knees. His eyes were closed and his head was bowed, massive paws beside his face. He was mouthing this phrase, "Father, bless this food to the nourishment of my body."

So it's like I told that crowd: You've got to be careful what you pray about.

I don't think there was anything we would do differently if we were preparing for that Cotton Bowl game again. Our workouts were well-organized and our build-up to game day was good. The only change I might have made would have been to bring a few more players. We brought sixty-eight and that left us a little short when we were setting up teams to give us a picture of what Penn State likes to do offensively and defensively. Penn State was a very difficult team to prepare for in a bowl game because they were so diversified and used a lot of motion we had seen little of during the season, when a majority of our opponents ran the wishbone offense. Still, we played good, solid football and at times we certainly played well enough to win. But at a time when we had to be a great team and shut folks down we gave up a touchdown in the third quarter and Penn State went back in front to stay. So we simply were beaten by a better football team on that day. Afterward everyone on both sides seemed to think it was a more competitive game than that final score of 41–20 indicated but that's the one that went in the record book, thanks to one of the craziest onside kickoffs in history.

I guess a lot of people thought Baylor, being entirely new to this type of game, might come out of the dressing room so fired up that we couldn't do anything. Actually, our emotional pitch was just about right. Some of the players were pretty tense when we reached the stadium that morning but everyone seemed more relaxed after Billy Graham appeared shortly before noon.

Dr. Graham had served as grand marshal for the Cotton Bowl Parade downtown that morning and then came to our dressing room wearing a new green and gold striped necktie. He congratulated us on being there to represent Baylor and then led us in a brief prayer. When he left there was a different atmosphere in the room.

It was an evenly-matched first half but we played a little more consistently than Penn State and made the only touchdown drive in the first quarter. Penn State settled down just before halftime and drove from their 14 to our 9 before kicking a field goal to make it 7–3. We led at halftime but we knew we were anything but secure.

In the dressing room I told our players, "They came off the field talking about how the fourth quarter is theirs, but you've controlled a lot of games in the fourth quarter, too." I think we went back out ready to play but Penn State's offense just came at us with more than we could handle, particularly after we lost Ken Quesenberry from our secondary.

Kenny played a marvelous game at safety until he went out with a knee injury in the third quarter. He already had made twelve tackles, seven of them unassisted, to give our front-line defense great support against Penn State's strong running attack and he was playing solid pass defense. Although he missed about a third of the game the media voted him the Outstanding Defensive Player, edging out Mike Hartenstine, Penn State's all-American defensive tackle. Joe Paterno said he really couldn't understand how that happened until he watched the game film and saw how much Kenny did for us that day. Then Joe agreed he deserved the award.

We were ahead when they helped him off the field but then very shortly we were behind. I think losing Kenny had a lot to do with it. He had experience back there and had been able to shut down some things they got away with later. Of course, Penn State had some fine offensive players. Tom Shuman proved to be a heck of a passer against us. Tom Donchez at fullback,

Jimmy Cefalo at flanker and Dan Natale, the tight end, were outstanding against us along with a lot of others. When it was over we could understand why Penn State had such a great reputation for playing in bowl games.

We had our moments, too. After Penn State went ahead 10–7 early in the third quarter we came back to make it 14–10. But then we faltered. On the second play Shuman hit Cefalo with a bomb and Penn State was on top again 17–14. Neal Jeffrey wasn't sharp that day but we felt he deserved to be playing for us. Then our offense stalled out for about ten minutes and the score went to 34–14. I replaced Neal with Mark Jackson. Mark looked good taking us 82 yards to score and make it 34–20 when Ricky Thompson caught his second touchdown pass of the afternoon. But then there was only fourteen seconds left in the game and I called for that onside kick.

A lot of people might not believe this but we worked on that play in practice all year long. Our plan was to kick the ball so that it took a good high bounce and hung in the air between the 50 and the Penn State 45, giving our coverage a chance to converge on it. When someone grabs the ball you blast him, the ball squirts loose and you have a chance for it. The only trouble was the kick came down about five yards short. Our players overran it and it was simple for a Penn State player to catch the ball and run 50 yards down an empty field to score. I just stood there stunned at the thought of pulling that on national television. I said to myself . . . well, I said, expletive deleted.

The game ended on that crazy note but I'm glad everyone remembered all the good things, not only after that day but the entire year. In the dressing room I told our players that they were champions who had lost to champions and that they always could be proud of what they achieved for Baylor. It was quiet in the room but no one was crying. I believe everyone realized that regardless of the score this game had been an important milestone for us.

There was another joint press conference three hours after the game and Paterno spoke graciously of Baylor's performance, including the onside kick.

"That was just one of those things," he said, "that

really shouldn't have happened. The way I see it, the onside kick at that stage of the game, when it was all over, was a tribute to Grant Teaff's thinking right up to the end.

"Baylor was simply a great team as far as I'm concerned. That late drive for a touchdown was big-league all the way and Baylor never quit out there.

"Baylor was no fluke. I have been very impressed by Grant Teaff and his team and I feel Baylor is here to stay. The way I see it the Southwest Conference is no longer a one-team conference.

"And let me say this: Grant is going to be one of the leaders in our profession for years to come."

Joe made me feel real good about our program but when I sat down in my hotel room with my family to watch the Orange Bowl game, I felt real dejected. Then I started looking at Alabama's situation—ranked Number One in the country with a perfect record coming into the Orange Bowl and then losing to Notre Dame. The announcers mentioned that was Bear Bryant's eighth straight loss in a bowl game. Suddenly I didn't feel as bad.

I told Donell, "Wouldn't it be wonderful to have a chance to lose eight bowl games in a row? You'd have a heck of a record if your teams kept going that far."

The next day I was feeling positive again, ready to devote all of my energy to recruiting. The Cotton Bowl game had settled into its proper place. I wanted desperately to win it and it hurt me deeply when we didn't but I understand there is more to life than materialistic things. My relationship with God is the important thing. If it is in balance it helps everything I do. The Cotton Bowl game was a great experience but I was ready now to look ahead. And the view was really exciting.

The American Football Coaches Association convened in Washington the next week and I was invited to speak on motivation. The coaches were very enthusiastic about my talk and I was pleased but I couldn't help wondering how they would mark their ballots in the AFCA's Coach of the Year election.

This was Tuesday and the winner would be announced on Thursday just before a huge Coach of the Year banquet.

I didn't think I'd have a chance since the voting came after the bowl games. I was one of eight nominees from various districts of the nation and John McKay, whose Southern Cal team had come back dramatically to beat Ohio State in the Rose Bowl, was another. But on Thursday afternoon they called me downstairs for a press conference. When I got back to the room I just walked in and hold Donell, "Hey, I won it!"

That night I sat on the dais with most of the great coaches I'd always admired. President Ford, who once coached at Yale while he attended law school and held membership in the AFCA for several years, was there to present the awards. I met him at the reception before the banquet and he was warm and friendly, a person who looked you in the eye and listened to you. When I was introduced as the national Coach of the Year and stepped up to receive my award from the President of the United States, I thought, "Man, this is a long way from Snyder, Texas!"

I told the crowd how special this award was to me and how thrilled I was to receive it, particularly since John McKay looked like such a strong threat. "I guess what swung the voting for me," I said, "was my expertise in coaching the onside kick."

The tributes were just beginning. There was Grant Teaff Day in Snyder, where Grant was saluted by old friends who had known him since boyhood. And there was Baylor Football Appreciation Night, a $25-a-plate dinner which attracted 1,300 people to the Waco Civic Center for one more round of rejoicing the Miracle on the Brazos.

Paterno proved his admiration for his rival coach and team was genuine by flying down from Pennsylvania in the midst of a busy recruiting season to be the evening's main speaker. He was beautiful. This was pigskin diplomacy at its best.

For a half hour Joe tossed out jokes, bouquets, and advice, all of which were accepted with glowing gratitude. When he finished, everyone was aroused. There was so much adrenalin pumping the Baylor players may have gone out in the parking lot and scrimmaged.

"I don't see why anyone should get carried away about who won our game," Paterno told them. He peered at different faces in the crowd and shrugged. "We play the game the next day and the score could flip, just like that.

"The real thrill of it is the chance to get ready for such a game, to participate and then coming off the field with some respect for each other."

Paterno reemphasized what he told Grant after the game.

"Don't let an exhibition game ruin a super season for you. You had a great football team—a bunch of young people who played football the way you like to see it played. You played with enthusiasm and poise. You were behind so often and you had enough courage and leadership to hang in there and win some games it looked like you couldn't possibly win. I think that's why everyone was caught up in your success. It not only was that you won but how you won.

"So you're up there. Now, there are goals out there just as important, just as challenging. And don't forget the thrill you had of striving. Don't ever forget that you'll never be happy just being content to go along.

"You guys who have gone through what you have and done what you've done, you have a great running leap at the world. So don't let up!"

After doing everything for Baylor pride short of enshrining the entire crowd in the National Football Hall of Fame, Paterno gave an encore. He rose with everyone else during the singing of "That Good Ol' Baylor Line," holding his right hand high in the bear claw sign so popular at Baylor.

It was delightful, an evening when nobody left empty-handed—or empty-hearted.

There were so many wonderful experiences during the months after I was elected Coach of the Year. I was on the move constantly, speaking at clinics and large banquets across the nation. So many people went out of their way to make me feel special. I wouldn't be truthful if I didn't say I enjoyed seeing myself in the papers and on television often and hearing my name wherever I went. I know this is not what life is all about but still it was very nice.

Then one afternoon during spring training at Baylor I was walking under the stadium, going back to my office to make a phone call. I was wearing my coaching clothes and I had on a gold jacket and a hat with BU on it. A young man walked up to me and asked, "Are you Don Oliver?"

"No, I'm not," I told him, "but I'll take you to his office."

He started walking with me but showed no sign of recognizing me. I thought he must be strange to all this. "Why do you want to see Mr. Oliver?" I asked him.

"It's about a sports story," he said. "I'm a sportswriter for *The Lariat*."

Well, I told myself, if he works on the campus paper he must have just transferred here from the University of Alaska. "Are you new at Baylor?" I asked him.

"Oh, no," he said. "I've been here three years."

I took him to Don's office and then left without saying a word. I made my phone call and then walked back out on the field. I stood there and watched the players in their drills, my feet very firmly on the ground.

14.
The Real Reward

When Grant Teaff was elected Coach of the Year by the American Football Coaches Association at their convention in Washington, he had an opportunity to meet the President of the United States at a reception preceding the awards banquet. Grant asked if he would autograph his banquet program and Gerald Ford gladly obliged.

When Grant and Donell returned home, she proudly showed the autographed program to their oldest daughter. Tammy, a seventeen-year-old high school senior, was impressed but not overwhelmed.

"Did he ask Daddy for *his* autograph?" she inquired.

This is typical of the devotion accorded the man of the house at 8265 Forest Ridge Drive in Waco. And Donell, his original cheerleader, emphasizes that it's mutual.

"His love for his daughters is as sweet, pure, and beautiful as anything I've ever seen," she said. "And it's a reciprocal thing, because they simply adore him. When he walks in the house it sort of lights up the world for all of us.

"Layne, who was nine years old when Baylor had that wonderful season in '74, is much like him because of her competitiveness. She covered her head with a blanket and cried the entire fourth quarter of the Cotton Bowl game. She simply could not stand to lose and, unlike her father, she had not yet learned to lose graciously.

"Tracy, who was fourteen at the time, has a very special thing with her father. I guess she is as much like him as any of the girls. In fact, she's much like a son would have been. She was a ball girl during Baylor's championship season and it was very special to her to be on the sideline near him.

"Tammy has a very open, understanding relationship with her father which is very gratifying for me to see. He uses the same approach with her that he uses with his players—honest but firm. His philosophy is if he's able to say yes he will, but if he can't he finds a satisfactory alternative. This worked very well with a daughter approaching college."

Despite the tremendous demands on his time, Grant always has remained close to his family. This was an area which athletic director Jack Patterson had feared might become a problem when Grant took the Baylor job in December of '71.

"I've seen some coaches so dedicated to their jobs that they forgot their families," Patterson said. "I told Grant I knew he probably would work 20 hours a day but always to find time for his youngsters while they were growing up. If he didn't he could lose his family.

"I told him he'd probably have more demands placed on him at Baylor than he would at, say, Texas Tech or A&M. Baylor people are jealous. If Grant appears at your Baptist church then others are offended if he doesn't appear at theirs. If Grant appears at the alumni meeting in Galveston, the people in Houston want him, too.

"I tried to tell him that Baylor people will impose too many demands, and some unusual demands, on his time *but* to be sure he found time for his family. Grant has done that. He has boundless energy. He can go with little rest. But he does isolate time for his wife and children. This is a real mark."

Donell noted, "There is a parallel between the discipline with his team and with his three daughters. Through the years his discipline has not come as a result of harsh, unkind, and screaming words. It's been a matter of motivating them so they want to do these things.

"A great part of his discipline has to be love. The players know he loves them. The coaches know he loves them. They want to do the job in order to please him.

"The players respond to him because of this and that's certainly the case with our girls, because they know he loves them and they respond. He cares and he expects the very best effort, the very best person that they can possibly be in every area of their life.

"Grant's not perfect. Nobody is. But he is for real. The priorities of his life, as I see them from my vantage point, are these:

"One, he wants to live his life as God would have him live it.

"Two, he wants to make his family happy and to raise his children as they should be raised. I believe this is why he tries to give them quality time.

"Three, he wants to fulfill his commitment to coach football and use it as an instrument with which to contribute to society and to the lives of young men."

Thus Grant has lived happily as a member of God's family while also becoming a successful father of two families of his own—the one at home and the one on the football field.

Whenever I speak at coaching clinics about the facets of a

successful career I always mention giving quality time to your family. It doesn't have to be long but when you're with them, concentrate. The worst thing you can do is say, "Well, I'm going to spend an hour with my family," and then go home and sit there thinking of football. Your children ask you something and you say, "Huh?" That's no way to treat them.

Look eyeball to eyeball with them, concentrate on what they're saying and communicate with them. It's amazing what one hour of quality time will do over ten hours of non-quality time.

Our family life is like a beehive in one way and it's a deep love affair in another. There are so many interests and activities demanding attention and exciting us and yet we never lose contact with the importance of loving and caring for each other.

Donell and I always have felt strongly that our daughters should develop character in every phase of their lives while they were growing up. We are very tough on them. They're disciplined, but they're disciplined through love.

No matter how puffed up one of the girls may get because I won't let her do something, before leaving my presence she says, "I love you, Daddy." And I say, "I love you. Now you remember that." I'll always remember how upset Tammy was when I refused to let her make an out-of-town trip with some other girls when she was a junior in high school. But a couple of days later I learned from an outside source that she told her friends at school, "I don't always understand the decisions my parents make but I know they make them because they love me. I'm proud that my mother and daddy are really tough on me."

That made me feel like a million dollars. She might gripe and fuss at me but it was a point of pride with her that we really did care and felt a genuine concern for her.

Once Tracy and Layne felt mighty low because they played on a terrible basketball team that didn't win any games, so I talked to them about setting goals. "If you have to face defeat, face it with the proper attitude," I told them, "and come away with something." So they set some goals.

Layne was so short she couldn't get the ball up to the basket so she played defense. She set a goal of stealing four balls per game and once she reached it she felt better. Tracy set a goal of scoring so many points per game and pretty soon she exceeded it. In the last game of the season she scored 31 points. So they felt a sense of accomplishment when it was over. We want them to strive for this in whatever they may do in life.

Just before we opened the season in '74 the equipment manager, Wally Wilson, asked me if it would be all right to ask a girl to be a ball person. We have four and we've used the sons of coaching staff members. There are two on each side of the field and each pair is responsible for six balls being available for play. It can become a pretty big job, particularly in wet weather. One person wipes a ball clean while the other is running on the field with a fresh one. Wally said he knew it would take a certain type of girl to run out on a field before 40,000 or 50,000 people and he thought Tracy would do a good job.

I was hesitant at first but Tracy was very excited about the idea. Then I began to think it might be good for her. She always worked on the Baylor side of the field and the first time she ran on the field with a ball she went past the huddle and a player stepped back on her foot. He looked at her and said, "Oh, my gosh, I'm sorry!" Tracy said, "That's okay!" and kept on running. She worked hard and took great pride in her job. After we won the Texas game she just flew into my arms. The photographers caught that scene and the picture received a lot of attention. That picture means a great deal to me because Tracy represented my entire family, sharing a very special moment.

After Penn State ran our onside kick back for a touchdown at the end of the Cotton Bowl game Layne was furious with Joe Paterno. She told her mother, "I'm going down to the Penn State locker room and kick that Coach Paterno on the leg." Donell tried to explain it was a fluke and it happened because of my decision. Later that night I was telling how gracious Joe had been to us at the press conference but Layne wasn't impressed. "He's a rat," she said. "He didn't mean those things." I said, "No, I think he did." "He's a rat," Layne said.

When Joe came to Waco to speak at our banquet several weeks later Layne, at my insistence, went very reluctantly. After the banquet I told her we were going to take Coach

Paterno back to his motel so he would be in the car with us. She said she'd ride with someone else. I told her she wouldn't and that she must get over this and get to know him.

Finally I took her up to Joe, turned her around to face him and introduced them. He started talking to her and was very gracious. I could tell the ice was breaking, but she still was tied up a bit.

When we got in the car, I said, "Layne was pretty upset about our game." Joe said, "Well, if we play again, Baylor will probably win it." Layne kinda liked that. By the time we got to the motel she asked him to sign her program.

Joe had brought us some gifts from Pennsylvania, including some chocolate from Hershey and a stuffed Nittany Lion for the girls. Layne was feeling quite warm toward him by the time we left.

On the way home, I said, "Now, Layne, you formed an opinion of a man based purely on the fact that we lost a football game. He's a pretty nice guy, isn't he?"

"He's nice," she said, "but next time we'll beat him, won't we?" I said, "Well, we'll try."

We've always had the girls in Sunday school and church. In the summer sometimes I would like to go to the lake or do something else but Donell has been the strong point in keeping us a disciplined church family. She's the most disciplined of all of us.

We try to teach them the importance of reading the Bible and the importance of spiritual development just like we would with an athlete. Or if I were in business I think I would take the same approach with my business associates, because it's a vital part of human existence. It can make you a happier individual and more fulfilled. But I try to be subtle. I think parents often make a big mistake by trying to cram Christianity down our children's throats.

In San Angelo our church turned the young people over to me one summer for the evening service. We had an innovative program at the lake. We'd water ski all afternoon, have snacks and then hold the church service. I think you have to be sharp in your method of getting Christian principles across to them. If you're not careful it becomes churchy and thus negative. Donell and I always have felt that by example our children could learn and grow in their Christian experience.

We certainly have our share of pranks, too. April Fool's Day is a real important time at our house. The girls look forward to it because they know we'll try to do something to catch them unaware. As the years passed this became increasingly difficult.

Once Donell's brother and sister-in-law, Rod and Marilyn Phillips of Lubbock, were expecting a baby on April 1 after hoping for a long time to have one. The girls knew Marilyn had taken the fertility drug and that this sometimes resulted in multiple births so we arranged for Donell's parents to call and say they'd had quadruplets, two boys and two girls. We managed to keep them believing this all day but that night I suggested we call Roddy and see how they were doing. Tammy was talking to him when I told her to ask to speak to Marilyn. While he called her to the phone a puzzled look came across Tammy's face. "What is Marilyn doing at home?" she asked. Then we yelled, "April Fool!"

Another time we set up all the clocks in the house so they would read 7:45 A.M. but actually go off at 3:00 in the morning. The girls thought they were late getting up for school and rushed around combing their hair and brushing their teeth. When they were ready they hurried outside and it was pitch dark. We laughed and told them what time it was and everybody went back to bed.

The most expensive joke was in 1974. Donell and I got up at 5:30 A.M. turned on every light in the house, made our bed and left the girls a note saying we were called to Dallas unexpectedly but for them to fix their breakfast and for Tammy to take everyone to school in her little Mustang. We turned the radio up full blast and hid in the closet.

They came downstairs to see what was happening and found the note. They looked all over the house for us, realizing what day it was. Finally they decided we really had gone so they set their alarm and got back to bed. When they did, we came out, hid the note, turned off all the lights, crawled back into our bed and set the clock-radio to come on in ten minutes.

When the girls came back downstairs they found us in bed and asked what we were doing there. We acted like they had lost their minds. They told us what had happened and I said they must have been dreaming.

We also had moved my car and Tammy's car from behind the house to in front of a neighbor's house down the hill. Tracy looked out and screamed, "The cars are gone!" We carried it a little further, saying we had left the keys in them the night before and they must have been stolen. This really upset them. Confusion was running rampant. Finally they got ready for school and Tammy went out front and saw our cars down the street. We yelled, "April Fool!" and they were pretty mad at us.

They were running a little late so they got in my car, which was parked behind Tammy's on the hillside. The windshield was fogged over and she couldn't see out when she got behind the wheel. She put it in neutral and the car rolled forward and hit her car. The collision completely caved in the grill of my car. Well, that cost me three hundred bucks. Some joke!

My coaching career has presented me with a great opportunity for outreach. I speak at coaching clinics and FCA gatherings as often as I possibly can because I want so much to share what I think has meaning to other lives.

When I speak to coaches I always stress the importance of goals.

"Define your goals," I tell them. "That's part of knowing where you want to go. If you want to be the head football coach at the University of Texas, write it down: in 1983 I want to be head football coach at the University of Texas. I want my office done in orange and white with a big picture of a longhorn over my desk. Draw it before you, visualize it, think about it, and work to attain it. I want you to go there because I want to still be at Baylor."

When I speak to FCA groups I constantly marvel at how you

can meet so many new friends on a common ground. In May of 1975 I received a letter which exemplified this:

> Dear Coach Teaff,
>
> Just a note to tell you how much I enjoyed what you had to say at the FCA banquet in Chicago last Thursday. It made a tremendous impression on me and I thought about "never giving in" many times last night during our game with Cleveland. We hung in there and won it 2–0 on a late inning home run.
>
> All of my teammates who were at the banquet really enjoyed your remarks and are still talking about that film.
>
> You're a real inspiration to coaches and athletes like myself and I wanted you to know I appreciate what you stand for on and off the field.
>
> Good luck to you and the Baylor Bears again this year.
>
> > Keep on keepin' on,
> > Jim Kaat

That was my first opportunity to know Jim Kaat, the Chicago White Sox pitcher. At the time of his letter he had won twelve straight games. He's undoubtedly a great athlete but I'll also remember him as a fine Christian.

"That film" was *The Athletes*, the story of our heartbreaking experience against TCU in '73 from which Neal Jeffrey and everyone at Baylor received such marvelous inspiration in '74. By the time I went to Chicago I had shown it at least a hundred times. I finally had managed to watch the entire film without crying.

> Grant and Donell frequently have the Baylor players visit their home, as do other members of the coaching staff. They believe it's an important part of their life while playing college football.
>
> "It's good for them to get out of the dormitory atmosphere and into a home occasionally," Donell

said. "They get to know the coaches and their families as people. At our house they can play pool, cards, dominoes, or other games. Or just sit around and visit awhile. This certainly is an advantage for coaches' wives because so often we know them only as numbers on the football field, and we don't like that.

"We like to know what they look like, who they are and how they talk. I think this has been very beneficial for everyone. I hope the players feel they can come to us any time they have a problem. Maybe they just need to have some help with their clothes, like having a button sewed on, or they simply need to sit in a den in someone's home and watch TV awhile.

"We visit them when they're in the hospital and sometimes we'll bring injured boys home with us for a day or so simply because they couldn't be cared for properly in a dormitory by themselves. Sure, they're big, tough guys out on the field but they're human beings, too. It's difficult for a boy of seventeen, or eighteen, being away from home and not having anyone right there to take care of you."

This "home away from home" concept is another key to the Teaff approach in relating with his players. They remember him for many reasons besides what he helped them accomplish on the football field.

"In my mind," said Neal Jeffrey, "he's the ideal coach. His faith is exactly like mine. He believes in God and wants to stand up and talk about it.

"He always been honest. I'm sure he's made mistakes. Who hasn't? But it seems he always had the answer when we needed one.

"His positive attitude toward everything did wonders for me. He was instrumental in my attacking my stuttering in a very positive way. I came so far from my freshman year when I first met him. When I was in high school I couldn't say a silent prayer without stuttering. He helped me so much to believe in myself and to grow.

"Coach Teaff has had an unbelievable effect on my life. Only my father has had a greater influence."

(James Neal Jeffrey Sr. played halfback for Baylor in the late '40s and became one of the pioneers in the Fellowship of Christian Athletes.)

"The spiritual atmosphere which Coach Teaff created at Baylor was beautiful to behold," Neal said. "He never crammed his faith down anyone's throat. He simply created an atmosphere in which, if you chose, you could grow, both as an athlete and as a believer.

"At Baylor we had our share of guys who were just as wild as anybody else. We also had those who felt strongly about their religion and wanted to speak out as Coach Teaff does. But he didn't push anybody. If you didn't share his beliefs, you knew he was open to talk about it. Everyone feels comfortable in his presence."

Steve Beaird noted, "Coach Teaff has a knack for motivation. It doesn't matter whether he's talking to the President of the United States or to someone in a slum area. He can talk to anybody and make them feel at ease. He's a motivator because he's serious in what he says. A lot of people talk just to be talking. I think because he's sincere and believes what he says then you have to believe it, too."

Aubrey Schulz declared, "He changed everything for me. I believe what he does about setting goals. In order to achieve any kind of success you have to work toward something. And when you're around him you want to strive for important goals. He's the best guy I've ever known."

Mark Jackson said, "I'm just thrilled to play under Coach Teaff. He's really been an influence on my life. Through him I motivate myself every day, not only on the football field but in my schoolwork and my other activities off the field. When I hear his name, I think of a winner—a winner in all aspects of life."

Derrel Luce observed, "I'm basically a cynical person. I don't expect to get too much from someone in authority in the way of freedom in decision-making or a fair deal in being able to tell your side of the story. But Coach Teaff gives you a good outlook on life because you can go in his office any time you want and talk to him. He won't always let you do what you want but he'll always listen to your views. That has had a marked effect on my life. That and the Christian atmosphere.

"Some people think that Christianity and football aren't compatible. They think an athlete has to be mean, bitter, and foul-mouthed. Some coaches kick and cuss players. Of course, Coach Teaff doesn't allow that. He tries to be constructive about everything and toward everybody. That's an outgrowth of his Christian approach to coaching and it helps a lot. You can't get anything out of a player by cussing or kicking him that you couldn't get out of him by encouraging him."

Alcy Jackson said, "I had an opportunity to attend a lot of colleges but after I spent thirty minutes with Coach Teaff I told him I was coming to Baylor. He gave me a warm handshake, a smile and put it on the line like he'd known me for a long time. I could feel the friendliness in him. He's the kind of guy you can get up and play for. It's amazing, the way he can affect his players.

"Sometimes we'll be out on the practice field and it's hot and we're starting to drag a little. He'll say, 'Whistle up a breeze' and we'll start whistling. And that breeze comes from somewhere. Maybe it was on its way in anyway, but that breeze comes from somewhere.

"He's the greatest man alive. I believe in him. He takes to all of us like we're his sons."

Through the years I've discovered one of the truly great re-

wards in coaching is found in the wonderful and lasting friend-
ships with which I have been blessed. Often I hear from
players whom I coached years earlier. They're well, happy,
and successful and they say they just want to thank me for
whatever I may have contributed to their growth.

In April of '75 I received a beautiful letter from Chester
Daughtery, a coach at Abilene Cooper High School who once
played for me at McMurry. I have read the closing paragraph
again and again.

Chester wrote, "With the exception of my parents and wife,
no other person has had the impact or influence on my life that
you have had. That is the reason we named our son John Grant.
We realized that the name does not make the man, but we
thought if by chance it did we wanted him to have a head start.
Thank you for being a part of my life."

I'll treasure that letter as highly as any Coach of the Year
plaque I may receive. It expresses what I always hope to accomplish with my life.

Seasons come and seasons go. Some are good and some are
bad. But I believe the thrill of sharing, loving, and growing in a
God-centered life reaches far beyond the won-loss record. I'll
cherish that forever.

FOR FURTHER READING

Beyond the Goal, *Kyle Rote, Jr. with Ronald Patterson*

Kyle Rote, Jr.—the amazing twenty-five-year-old powerhouse who won ABC's 1974 and 1976 Superstar competitions—tells how he keeps in shape . . . why he views soccer as "the global game" . . . what he thinks of professional sports, coaches, and teammates. A fast-moving, action-packed story of a genuine, home grown, 100% American Superstar. No. 80390 (hardback).

The Real Score, *Gene Littler with Jack Tobin*

The heroic comeback of Gene "The Machine" Littler—million-dollar golf champion . . . victim of cancer. In 1972 radical surgery removed the essential muscle structure of Gene's left arm and side. But fifteen months and nineteen days later he was back among the winning pros and on his way to greater success than he had ever known!

First Down, Lifetime to Go, *Roger Staubach with Sam Blair and Bob St. John*

The Dallas Cowboys' 1976 Superbowl quarterback gives you an intimate look into his life. Why he chose four years of active Navy duty and risked missing forever the riches of pro ball . . . how he managed to keep a clear head on the field while his mother was dying . . . what it's like to win every major award that can be given to a professional football player. No. 80380 (hardback).

They Call Me Coach, *John Wooden with Jack Tobin*

The fascinating first-person story of John Wooden, the brilliant coach who built a basketball dynasty at UCLA that spanned four decades. "Coach" traces his career from being an All-American guard to coaching championship teams that have rocked the sports world

. . . and reveals his philosophy on how to coach and build champions. A rare inside look at a remarkable man. No. 90045 (paperback).

Gary Player World Golfer, *Gary Player with Floyd Thatcher*

Gary Player—what qualities make him so often a winner? What are the secrets of his physical fitness? How did he cure his hook? Read this exciting life-story and be prepared to grow as a golfer . . . or just as a person searching for success and fulfillment in your own life and work. No. 80359 (hardback).

Third Base Is My Home, *Brooks Robinson with Jack Tobin*

How did Brooks Robinson achieve his spectacular success? Baseball's "Mr. Nice Guy" tells his story from sandlot struggler to major league superstar. You'll share insights into his heartwarming philosophy of life . . . his profound love for his family and his deep personal faith. A "must" for baseball buffs, and full of human interest for all. No. 80330 (hardback).

A Year At a Time, *Walter Alston with Jack Tobin*

A fascinating, inside look at Walter Alston, manager of the Los Angeles Dogers. Here, in his own words, is the side of Walter Alston most people never see, the side that doesn't make the sports page of the headlines, including his unique perspective on baseball and its role in life from the vantange point of over forty years' association with the game. No. 80413 (hardback).

The Gift of Wholeness. *Hal L. Edwards.*

The warmly human story of a modern pilgrim in search of himself . . . and in search of God. A refreshing look at one minister and his ministry—a vulnerable, open kind of life that grows and keeps on growing. No. 80377 (hardback).

Barefoot Days of the Soul. *Maxie D. Dunnam.*

Remember when you were a child how you longed for the first warm days of spring when your mother finally let you go barefoot? How marvelous and free it felt. "Nothing in my experience, says Maxie Dunnam, "is more suggestive of the promise of the gospel than that. This book is about freedom. It's a thank-you celebration—an invitation to barefoot days of the soul." No. 80432 (hardback).

The One and Only You. *Bruce Larson.*

People don't come in carbon copies. We may accept that idea, but how do we make the most of being one of a kind? Bruce Larson is convinced that every one of us unique "yous" has an unlimited potential to draw on—the liberating security of God's love. Here he probes what that can mean for us and gives us practical ways of putting our potential to work. No. 91012 (A Key-Word paperback).

Let God Love You. *Lloyd John Ogilvie.*

In thirty-eight devotional meditations, the author takes the struggles of life seriously and turns them into stepping stones to Christian growth. Paul's letter to the Philippians forms the basis for these refreshing thoughts. No. 80353 (hardback).

The Becomers. *Keith Miller.*

A helpful and insightful look at what happens to a person after he or she becomes a Christian. Realistic, honest, and full of hope, for people who "are in the process of becoming whole as we reach out with open

and creative hands toward work, people, and God."
No. 80321 (hardback).

Habitation of Dragons. *Keith Miller.*

"Miller is forceful, witty, honest and surprising in his interpretation of a Christian life style. [Here] we have a combat diary for people trying to enlarge on the spiritual dimensions of existence"—David Poling, *New York Times.* Divided into forty-two selections, *Habitation of Dragons* is a book to be lived with one day at a time. No. 80182 (hardback). No. 91010 (A Key-Word book).

Come to the Party. *Karl A. Olsson.*

An invitation to a celebration of life. God invites us to his party, but some of us are like the older brother—we look on from the outside, knowing the party is not for us—we are not free to accept the love and blessing of our Father. Learn with Karl Olsson how to enter into a freer life style, secure in the love of God. No. 80296 (hardback). No. 98001 (paperback).

Enjoy the Journey. *Lionel A. Whiston.*

Accepting the fact that God loves us in spite of our failures, understanding our fellow man, and facing up to moral responsibility are just a few of the keys to a fuller spiritual life which Lee Whiston discusses in his warm and personal way in this helpful book. No. 80250 (hardback).

The Edge of Adventure: An Experiment in Faith.
Keith Miller and Bruce Larson.

Discover the difference Christian commitment can make in your job and your vocation; in your involvement in the church; in overcoming guilt, fears, anxiety, loss of faith, loneliness, depression. Life can become an adventure. No. 98026 (paperback); No. 40088 (leader's guide); No. 40089 (study guide); CRC-0627 (13-week cassette study course).

Living the Adventure: Faith and Hidden Difficulties.
Keith Miller and Bruce Larson.

For Christians who are already "beyond the edge" and are now striving to live the adventure. Honest but hopeful insight into the difficulties that are part of living as a Christian—confession and forgiveness, money and possessions, Christian sexuality, loneliness, success, change and growth, sickness and death, and more. No. 98055 (hardback); No. 40103 (leader's guide); No. 40104 (study guide); CRC-0633 (13-week cassette study course).